Sarum Chronicle

recent historical research on Salisbury & district

Issue 13: 2013

Salisbury Community Choir singing in the City Hall in Cape Town with three South African choirs. Author's collection.

Contents

How to contact us:
To order a copy of the current edition phone Ruth Newman on 01722 328922
or email ruth.tanglewood@btinternet.com

Copies of issues 1–10 are available at the price of £3 per copy, or £25 for the
set, plus postage at cost. Please contact Jane Howells on 01722 331426 or email
as below.

To submit material for consideration in future editions e-mail Jane Howells at
jane@sarum-editorial.co.uk with the words Sarum Chronicle in the subject line.

Editorial Team: John Chandler, John Elliott, Jane Howells, Sue Johnson, Ruth
Newman, David Richards and Margaret Smith.

Editorial

L ast year's editorial expressed the hope that a *Sarum Chronicle* lecture would become an annual event. We are pleased to say that this did happen; on a cold November evening, Professor Caroline Dakers, using untapped family archives, kept us enthralled with her talk on the Morrisons of Fonthill. Her paper in this issue concentrates on the impact of the Morrisons since 1829 with an emphasis on the buildings of the estate.

Other contributions cover a time range from medieval to modern. The contents demonstrate the huge variety of topics of interest to local historians; and allow our readers to appreciate the wealth of sources available locally, and the fascination and enjoyment that research generates.

Over the years in the life of Sarum Chronicle we have established a pattern, not always strictly enforced, of including an article that celebrates an anniversary and something on buildings being renovated or an area being redeveloped. We believe it is essential to recognise that Salisbury is both the city and cathedral, and aspects – sometimes the minutiae – of the history of both always appear. Salisbury has never functioned in isolation, and the '& district' part of the sub-title is very important to the journal.

2013 saw the publication of the latest volume in our *Sarum Studies* series – *Harnham Historical Miscellany*, a tribute to the late Michael Cowan, author of articles in issues 4 and 8 of *Sarum Chronicle*. See inside the back cover for further information.

With additional pages and extra colour sections the journal is reaching a wider audience than ever before, able to share the delights of our region's rich history. As ever we need your support to ensure our future existence – so please contact us if you have a piece of research on the Salisbury area which would make a suitable article, even a short note, or if you would be interested in reviewing a local book for us. We would also value your comments and feedback. Let us know if there is any topic you would like to read about, though no promises that we can find an author! Do tell your friends about *Sarum Chronicle* and encourage them to buy a copy.

The Diocesan Registry where Henry and Thomas worked. Henry eventually became Chief Clerk. EY28

An Art Gallery for Salisbury

Sue Johnson

In February 1912 readers of Salisbury's local newspapers received the news that the city was to be given a collection of local paintings, a purpose built gallery to house them and an endowment to pay for their upkeep. The donor was a local artist Edwin Young, who for over 30 years had been recording scenes in and around the city.

FAMILY

Edwin was one of at least 13 children of Isaac Young, shoemaker, and Mary Ann Randell Sutton, who married on 20 January 1818 at St Edmund's church, Salisbury. Isaac was described as 'of Southampton' and so far nothing has been discovered about his parentage. Mary was the youngest daughter of William Sutton, clothier, of Salisbury.[1] The frequent changes of address revealed in the baptism records of their children, together with Isaac's award of a ten year interest free loan only given to poor young men, and an appearance in court as an insolvent debtor[2] do not suggest a prosperous family background. When Edwin and his brother Henry were baptised at St Martin's church on 27 March 1831 they were living in Barnard Street.

In late 1833 or early 1834 the family moved to the Canal/Butcher Row area when Isaac's tender of £90 per annum to operate the city's weighbridge was accepted. Much used by vehicles coming to the market, a fee was charged for each load weighed, the tenant hoping that revenue would substantially exceed the amount they had paid to the Directors & Trustees of Highways to operate it. The weighbridge, facing the Canal, backed onto the watch-house for the city's constables in Butcher Row, and it was a condition that 'the tenant do officiate as perpetual constable.' Following an inspection both the watch-house and the weighbridge were found to be in a bad state of repair, and in March 1834 a bill of £12 19s for expenses incurred by Mr Isaac Young 'in consequence of the untenable state' of the watch-house was referred to committee. It was subsequently rejected, though he was allowed £5 on account of his rent.[3] In 1836 when the city police force was created Isaac was no longer a constable but the Watch Committee resolved that 'The duties of Billet Master be for the present performed by Isaac Young'.[4] Exactly what this entailed is not specified, presumably he had to look after the accommodation for the constables and attend to any prisoners kept overnight in the cells before being brought up before the magistrates. The existing provision for the new police force was declared to be inadequate and, following the abandonment of plans for a completely new building on the grounds of cost, it was decided that the Directors of Highways would give up the house and premises usually occupied by the lessee of the 'weighing engine' except for a small counting room in the front. This was to be blocked off from the rest of the building and adaptations made so that the Superintendant of Police could reside there and perform the duties of Billet Master.[5]

The Young family were on the move once again, but this time probably only a short distance away as their address is subsequently still given as 'Woodmarket'. Things took another turn for the worse a few months later when the latest additions to the family, twin boys named Walter and Frank, died in June when they were only a month old. In September came another blow – the death of Isaac at the age of 49, 'after a long and painful illness'.[6] He left seven children under 15, Edwin being just 8 years old at the time. Following Isaac's death Mary Young continued as tenant of the weighbridge until 1850. After losing the tenancy the family were living in Brown Street by 1851, Ox Row ten years later, and then Queen Street, where Mary died in 1870. She must have been a very strong-willed lady to keep her family together after her husband's death. The census returns perhaps give a hint of this – in 1851 and 1861 she is described as the

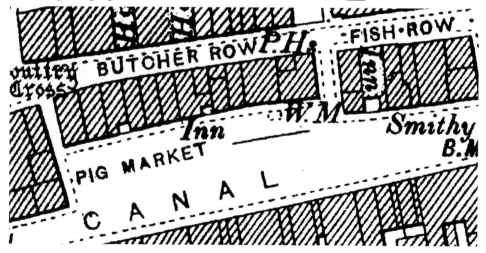

Extract from 1:2500 OS map, 1901. The position of the weighbridge is indicated by W.M.

Wood-Market, Salisbury

ISAAC YOUNG, BOOT and SHOEMAKER, impressed with a due sense of gratitude to those Friends who have for a number of years honoured him with their Favours, begs leave to inform them, that having, from *unforeseen circumstances*, been compelled to leave his former Residence, he has taken a SHOP in the WOOD-MARKET, where he trusts, by punctuality and despatch, to carry on his Business, in all its branches, with the utmost satisfaction to all those who may be pleased to favour him with their Orders.

N.B. - All Goods manufactured with the *best* Materials, and at the *lowest* possible Prices.
SEPTEMBER 13, 1838.   [7264

Advert in *Salisbury and Winchester Journal,* 17 September 1838, p4

head of the household even though her oldest son Henry was over 21 and would normally have had that title.

CAREER

Of Edwin's eight surviving siblings Clarissa died three years after her father in 1841,[7] Mary and Eliza married and Sarah Maria kept house for her brothers after their mother's death for a time, but then seems to have suffered some sort of illness or injury as she is described as an 'imbecile' in 1881. None of the boys took up their father's occupation as shoemakers but all worked at first as some kind of clerk - had they perhaps honed their writing and arithmetic skills by helping out with the weighbridge? Henry and Thomas worked in the Probate Registry in The Close, with Thomas later becoming a music seller before retiring. William was an accountant and land agent and Herbert, described as an accountant in 1871, later became a hosier - the 'Young' of Eldridge & Young, Catherine Street, a well known Salisbury shop.

Edwin was not at home in the 1851 census - the only person of the correct age and birthplace is at Winchester in the Diocesan Training College for School Masters, then located in Wolvesey Palace. Surviving records are scanty, but do reveal that Edwin's first post was St Thomas's School, Salisbury.[8] A daily school had been established in 1832 but did not have purpose built premises, being accommodated in 'a small ill-ventilated [room] above the Vestry of the Church'.[9] No early admission registers or log books survive but in 1859 there were 60 boys at the school, possibly a similar number had been there when Edwin Young was appointed at a salary of £50 per annum on 19 March 1852 when he was said to be a former pupil of the school.[10] The next five annual meetings continued his employment on the same terms but in 1857 no meeting is recorded, and in 1858 someone else is 're-elected', with no mention at all being made of him. Fortunately the *Salisbury Journal* is a little more informative, revealing that Mr Young had resigned, that the School Committee had passed a resolution commending his efficiency during his five years as master, and voted a sum of money for a suitable testimonial. His pupils had apparently been equally appreciative 'on Monday evening last an elegant silver butter knife was presented to him by the boys who attend the school'.[11] In 1861 Edwin was described as a 'Land Agent & Surveyor's Clerk', before becoming, like William, an accountant. He was for some years connected with Messrs Rigden's estate agency business.[12] By 1891 he was 'Living on his own means' and ten years later his occupation is given as 'Landscape Painter'.

LEISURE

Salisbury's Literary & Scientific Institute was founded in 1850 and by 1851 had about 400 members.[13] No membership lists survive but it is possible that Edwin Young and his brothers were among the 400 – the committee minutes of 1854 note that a letter had been received from a Mr Young 'recommending two educational serials' and alongside the list of committee members retiring later that year are some names in pencil, including 'E. Young'.[14] 'Mr Young' continues on the committee for a number of years and by 1858 there is also an H Young, possibly Edwin's brother Henry. In 1864 Edwin became Assistant Secretary and in the years following the names of Edwin Young and Alfred Watson, joint Hon Secretaries appear in adverts for lectures and entertainments organised by the Institute.[15] In September 1868 both declined to continue due to other commitments. However in the absence of any other candidates Edwin was persuaded to stay on for a further year 'at considerable inconvenience'. On being thanked for his services he modestly said that it had given him a great deal of pleasure to serve the institution and that 'if anything he had done had tended in the slightest degree to the benefit and prosperity of the institution he was sufficiently rewarded for his services.' He was succeeded by Mr William Young – a proposal carried by acclamation – who had 'been more or less connected with the institution for 13 years'.[16] Edwin continued as a committee member, but for exactly how long has not been established as no minutes survive after 1859. When the institute decided that it needed a new home Mr E Young and Mr Watson were two members of the building committee, appointed on 17 December 1869, and then became trustees of the new premises.[17] Edwin was also a founder member of the Salisbury Church of England Church School Institute.[18]

32 HIGH STREET

The unmarried Young brothers stayed together in the family home until at least 1871, when they were living at 2 Queen Street (the Guildhall side, near the corner with the Canal). Thomas married in 1874 and it was perhaps this which prompted the others to move - by 1881 they are living at 32 High Street. This was a large building on three floors. The front portion was a shop, while the living accommodation had drawing, dining, breakfast and morning rooms, seven bedrooms, servants' bedrooms, principal and back staircases, kitchen, scullery, wash-house etc. The gardens ran down to the river Avon, and it was here that Edwin had his 'brick and tile studio, 14ft. 6in. by 9ft. 6in.'[19] The building was demolished in 1976 but a picture of its fine staircase appears in the Royal Commission inventory of buildings of historic interest and a glimpse of the interior is found in adverts for the Blue Bird Cafe which it subsequently became.[20]

Some time between 1881 and 1891 William married and moved out. Henry died in March 1910 and William a few months later[21] leaving 32 High Street, which he owned, to Edwin, who continued to live there for the rest of his life. William also left his share of houses in Clarendon Terrace, which he owned jointly with Edwin, to him. The 1911 census describes the household at 32 High Street as Edwin himself, a gentleman of private means, with his housekeeper, Mrs Britten, her husband (occupation: 'carpenter & man-nurse'), their two children and a young lady assistant in the dairy which occupied the shop premises.

EDWIN THE ARTIST

No information has been discovered about how the son of a shoemaker came to be an accomplished artist. One possible influence was Richard Cockle Lucas, the son of his mother's older sister, Martha. Lucas was a sculptor (his works include the statue of Sir Richard Colt Hoare in Salisbury Cathedral) who studied in the Royal Academy Schools, and who came into contact with some of the finest artists of the day including Turner and Constable. He was considerably older than Edwin, but his son Albert Durer Lucas, also an artist, was just three years younger.[22] Edwin's earliest surviving painting is 'Common Friends', a copy of 'Rustic Scene' by Robert Hillis, dated 1849. It was said to be 'about the first of his attempts that he felt to be worth preserving'. His style was described in the local papers at the time as reminiscent 'of the famous Birket Foster', who was a painter, illustrator, engraver and member of the Royal Watercolour Society.[23] A modern

Part of St Thomas's graveyard. Edwin's father and three brothers who died as children were buried at this church. EY351

opinion is that he was 'a competent and prolific Victorian watercolourist - the best of his work being fine examples of the genre'. In 1962 'A view from Milford Bridge' and 'The Cathedral Spire from Stratford-sub-Castle' were borrowed by the Russell-Cotes Art Gallery in Bournemouth to form part of their 'Painters of Wessex' exhibition.[24] The majority of surviving paintings are watercolours, but he also worked in oils, exhibiting at the Bath & West Show when it was held at Salisbury in 1866 and 1867. In 1866 his 'Meadows, Harnham' was described as 'a very pleasing and naturally painted picture' and was priced at £15 15s. The following year 'Landscape - View from the Butts, looking towards Salisbury' was said to be 'a very clever picture... very creditable to the painter, who is only an amateur, and not a professional artist.' [25] Analysis of the dated items in the only known list of works shows that the bulk are from the 1890s/1900s, obviously when Edwin was well enough off to devote much time to his hobby. Although in failing health Edwin's interest in art continued to the end of his life and he produced at least one painting in 1911 - of the yard of the Crown Inn just a few doors away in the High Street.[26] Unfortunately this cannot be identified among surviving paintings in the Edwin Young Collection.

Art Gallery for Salisbury

THE PICTURE GALLERY

In February 1912 the City Council learned of Edwin Young's intention to donate his collection of 'about 200 water colour drawings, about 100 of which were newly mounted and framed by him for the purpose of the gift and the other 50 [sic] would be placed in a book interleaved with descriptive verses.' He would also provide a suitable building to house the collection, and as an endowment 'would at once convey by deed of gift to the Town Council 4 houses in Clarendon Terrace.' The income from these was to cover the cost of exhibiting the pictures and the balance devoted to purchasing works of arts for the proposed gallery. In the meantime the pictures would be on display in the Free Library. The Council unanimously passed a resolution thanking Mr Young and expressing their appreciation of his 'patriotism and citizenship'.[27]

By 8 March 130 water colours had been placed in the Library's Reading Room, 'chiefly of rural scenes in the immediate vicinity of Salisbury', many of them the meadows around Harnham. A 'complete list of the pictures already hung' completed the article. A month later the second batch of pictures was added, bringing the total to over 200 - again listed in the *Salisbury Times* - and the Council increased the insurance on them while they were in the Library to £600.[28] Alderman Haskins was much concerned in the matter, spending time writing the descriptions on the backs, so that they might label them later on', and with the Mayor and Chairman of the General Purposes Committee forming one of the sub-committee appointed to liaise with the architect about the new gallery.[29] No proper catalogue of the pictures ever seems to have been produced. The lists in the newspaper contain 201 items, though nothing is written against number 138, and there must have been another six items as later official documents clearly refer to 207 water colour drawings by Edwin Young but no information about these has been found.[30]

A site for the new gallery adjacent to the recently opened Public Library in Chipper Lane was purchased in May 1912 and in June the plans submitted to

The Edwin Young Collection is now housed in the Salisbury Library building. It is a registered charity, number 309519, whose aim is to advance the education (including aesthetic education) of the public by establishing and maintaining for exhibition to the public a collection of watercolours, paintings, prints and drawings which are of artistic merit or historical or topographical interest and in particular watercolours, paintings, prints and drawings of Salisbury and the neighbourhood thereof. Items in the collection can be seen on www.wiltshiretreasures.org

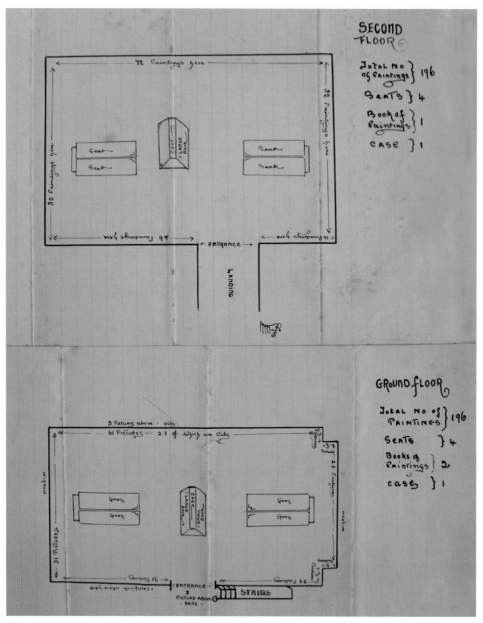

The total number of paintings comes to 391 (of which 28 were oils) plus 3 books of paintings. G23/894/4 (part)

the Council were passed. They show a single room on the ground floor, lit by tall windows at the front, and sloping rooflights at the rear, with the upper floor also having a large 'lantern' in the centre of its high ceiling.[31] Both rooms were panelled. The architect was Mr G L Blount, possibly a personal friend as the 1911

The gallery in Chipper Lane, now offices. Photograph by the author 2013. The inscription reads: This gallery was built AD 1913 and presented by Edwin Young citizen of Salisbury to the Mayor and Corporation together with upwards of 300 original drawings by the donor of picturesque buildings and places of natural charm in the neighbourhood of Salisbury to form the nucleus of an art collection and made free to the city by an accompanying endowment.

Kelly's Directory gives his address as 39 High Street, the builders were Messrs Chivers of Devizes, though most men who worked on the building were from Salisbury, Mr Ernest Usher provided the furniture, and Mr Frank Uphill the picture frames.[32] The only information about the internal layout of the gallery found so far is an undated floor plan drawn on two sheets of notepaper showing two rooms each with four seats, one display case in the centre and paintings all round the walls. Whether this was the actual layout or merely a suggested one is not clear, but it would be a logical design.

Unfortunately Edwin Young did not live to see his Picture Gallery completed, dying on 22 March 1913 just a few weeks before it was finished. He was buried at London Road cemetery after a funeral service, which was, in accordance to his wishes 'of a very simple character'.[33] His brother Thomas, one of his executors, completed the project and presented a further 181 framed pictures plus a number in three bound volumes, though it is not clear whether these were all by Edwin Young or not,[34] nor whether Edwin put the pictures into 'volumes' himself or if it was done after his death by Thomas. No list of these additional items has been found.

Once the gallery was finished the date for the official opening was set for 28 July 1913. This was subsequently postponed due to delays in finalising the legal transfer of the property to the Council and instead the Gallery seems to have simply opened its doors quietly to the public on the set date.[35] There was, however, one event to mark the construction of the building – a dinner given by Thomas Young at the Assembly Rooms (now Waterstones) for those who had worked on the project when it was nearing completion. After a meal and various speeches the evening was rounded off with a selection of songs![36]

Sue Johnson is a local historian with a particular interest in early Victorian Salisbury. She has been researching Edwin Young since reading a newspaper article in 1994.

Acknowledgments
Items from the Salisbury City Council and Picture Gallery archives are reproduced by kind permission of the Wiltshire and Swindon History Centre. Images from the Edwin Young Collection are reproduced by kind permission of the Trustees.

Bibliography and Notes
Abbreviations
SJL = *Salisbury & Winchester Journal/Salisbury Journal* STM = *Salisbury Times*
Bath and West of England Society, 1866, *Catalogue of pictures* [in the Bath & West Society archive at Bath University] (1866 catalogue)
Bath and West of England Society, 1867, *A catalogue of oil paintings, drawings and sketches etc., in the Arts Department, Salisbury, 1867* (1867 catalogue)

Crittall, Elizabeth (ed), 1962, *Victoria County History, Wiltshire,* Volume 6 (VCH6)
Little, Monte, ?1981, *Libraries in Salisbury 1850-1922,* thesis [unpaginated]
RCHM, 1980, *Ancient and historical monuments in the city of Salisbury,* 1, HMSO
OS map 1901, 1:2500 Second Edition, sheet Wilts 66:15

Internet resources accessed 2013
www.measuringworth.com
www.Charity-Commission.gov.uk

At the Wiltshire and Swindon History Centre
776/220, Sale Particulars 32 High Street, 1913
1900/43, St Thomas Sunday School committee minute book 1827-85
A1/950, Quarter Sessions Small Debtors Court, minutes of proceedings 1824-47
F8/600/233/7/27/1, Salisbury St Thomas C of E School Misc papers 1815-99
G23/1/24, City Council minutes 1822-33
G23/1/90, Directors & Trustees of Highways minutes 1827-43
G23/1/91, Directors & Trustees of Highways minutes 1843-52
G23/100/19, City Council minutes 1911-12
G23/100/20, City Council minutes 1912-13
G23/111/1, Watch Committee minutes 1836-60
G23/132/16, Clerk's Correspondence Files, Young Picture Gallery 1915-69
G23/132/20, Clerk's Correspondence Files, Salisbury Library, 1910-1974
G23/132/248, Guildhall and other Council owned pictures 1937-74
G23/894/4, Librarian's Correspondence: Edwin Young Collection 1957-74
G23/993/1, Salisbury Literary & Scientific Institute Committee minutes 1852-56
G23/993/2, Salisbury Literary & Scientific Institute Committee minutes 1856-59
G23/993/4, Salisbury Literary & Scientific Institute letters & papers 1850-60

Census [entries relating to Edwin are underlined]
1841 <u>HO107/1190/7/f31</u>
1851 HO107/1847/f67 & 221; <u>HO107/1674/f286</u>
1861 <u>RG9/1316/f49</u>; RG9/1316/f42
1871 <u>RG10/1953/f57</u>; RG10/1952/f76
1881 <u>RG11/2071/f10</u>; RG11/2071/f54; RG11/2072/f74; RG11/1179/f46
1891 <u>RG12/1620/f7</u>; RG12/1617/f77; RG12/1618/f15; RG12/1618/f25
1901 <u>RG13/1954/f9</u>; RG13/1952/f154; RG13/1952/f158
1911 <u>RG14 PN12116 RG78PN679 RD253SD3 ED13SN49</u>; RG14 PN12106 RG78PN679
   RD253SD3 ED3SN248

Notes
1   SJL 1870 Sep 17, p8
2   G23/1/24, 23 Sep 1824; SJL 1832 Jly 09, p3; A1/950, 31 Jly 1832
3   G23/1/90, 06 & 20 Sep 1833; 21 Mch 1834
4   VCH6, p113; G23/111/1, 19 Feb 1836
5   G23/111/1, 04 Feb 1837; 30 Mch 1837; 21 Mch 1838
6   St Thomas's register of burials, 17 Jne & 18 Sep 1839; SJL 1839 Sep 16, p4

7   SJL 1841 Sep 06, p4. A sister Martha had died 1828, age 14, buried 2 Mch St Edmund and a brother William Henry age 2 in 1825, buried 27 Jly, St Edmund

8   Hampshire Record Office 47M91/W/D1/1 Students Register 1840-72

9   appeal leaflet for new school in F8/600/233/7/27/1

10 VCH6,163; 1900/43

11 SJL 1857 Apl 25, p3

12 STM 1913 Mch 28, p5

13 VCH6, 143

14 G23/993/1, 05 Jan & 15 Jne 1854

15 SJL 1864 Oct 22, p5; SJL 1865 Oct 07, p5

16 SJL 1869 Sep 11, p7

17 SJL 1870 Nov 26, p6

18 Little; SJL 1869 Jly 24

19 SJL 1876, Oct 14, p4; 776/220

20 RCHM p66-68, plate 88, monument 77; 1938 Official *Town Guide*, p131. The site is now occupied by the Cheltenham & Gloucester Bank

21 STM 1910 Mch 26, p8 [Henry]; Nov 25, p8 [William], whose will was proved 2 Apl 1911, estate £47,448 (more than £3,000,000 at today's value)

22 Richards, David, 2008, Richard Cockle Lucas 1800-1883. *Sarum Chronicle*, 8, p51-57

23 STM 1912 Mch 08, p7; Myles Birket Foster 1825-99, *Dictionary of British Art vol IV, Victorian Painters*, Vol 1, Christopher Wood, 1995, Antique Collectors Club, p178

24 www.culture24.org.uk; letters 11 Apl, 2 May, 4 May, 5 Jly 1962 in G23/132/248

25 SJL 1866 Jne 09, supplement; 1866 Catalogue (in the same exhibition Louise Rayner's 'Market Scene, Chippenham' was priced at £18 18s); SJL 1867 Jne 15, supplement; 1867 Catalogue

26 STM 1912 Mch 08, p7 & Apl 26, p7; SJL 1913 Mch 19, p5

27 STM 1912 Feb 02, p8

28 STM 1912 Mch 08, p7; Apl 26, p7; May 03, p8

29 SJL 1912 Feb 03, p7 & Apl 06, p7

30 IR69/604, death duty, at The National Archives

31 G23/150/151, 21 Chipper Lane deeds, EY paid £325 for the site; G23/100/19, General Purposes Committee, 20 Jne 1912; plan in G23/132/20

32 STM 1913, Jne 27, p8; SJL 1913, Jne 28, p5; Kelly's Directory of Wiltshire 1911, Ernest Usher, cabinet maker, 42 Salt Lane; Frank Uphill, picture frame maker, 12 Winchester St; sketch plan in G23/894/4

33 SJL 1913 Mch 29, p5. His will, made 8 June 1912 contains no reference to the Gallery, only bequests to family and friends. His estate was £10,841 12s 5d, more than £800,000 at today's value

34 1915 conveyance in G23/132/16; letter to Ministry of Education 9 Apl 1957 in G23/894/4, stating that Thomas Young presented 'a number of pictures (for the most part painted by Edwin Young) and certain furniture and fittings'

35 G23/100/20, 3 Jly & 7 Aug 1913; STM 1914, Jne 05, p8; STM 1915, Jan 08, p5 & Feb 05, p8. The legal formalities were not completed until January 1915. By then the Gallery had been open to the public for more than a year, and the country was at war, so by agreement with Thomas Young no official ceremony took place.

36 STM 1913, Jne 27, p8; SJL 1913 Jne 28, p5

Some restorations of Salisbury Cathedral: the work of James Wyatt and George Gilbert Scott

John Elliott

James Wyatt (1746–1813), was the sixth son of Benjamin Wyatt who was a prosperous Staffordshire farmer, timber merchant, and builder. Wyatt senior trained his sons in the family building business. However, James showed signs of artistic talent and was sent to Italy to study the architecture of antiquity and the Renaissance. He visited Venice and then Rome and spent six years in Italy before returning to Britain around 1768. What he learnt while in Italy enabled him to become one of the most fashionable architects of the late 18th century. John Thorpe, the English Jesuit, wrote to Lord Arundell at Wardour Castle, Wiltshire, claiming that Wyatt 'was esteemed to have the best talents for Architecture of any of our countrymen who for several years has been in Rome'.[1]

On his return to Britain, Wyatt designed the Pantheon in Oxford Street, a place of public entertainment. His designs were exhibited at the Royal Academy in 1770 and he was much praised when the building opened in 1772. The rotunda was one of the largest rooms that had been built in England up to that time and had a central dome that was similar to the Pantheon in Rome.[2]

Wyatt was a great traveller and is reputed to have covered about 4,000 miles a year. His fees were 5% of the value of the work done, plus 2/6d (12.5p) a mile for travelling expenses and £5 guineas (£5.25) for a site visit. A site consultation without a contract was charged at £10 guineas (£10.50). He maintained a large London office.

Apparently Wyatt was not a good businessman and regularly over committed himself, something that caused his clients to get irritated. In May 1809 'Wyatt's conduct in neglecting Lord Pembroke's alterations at Wilton ... [meant that] Lord Pembroke had given him up, his patience having been exhausted'.[3] A few years later, in 1812 William Beckford at Fonthill complained about the 'utter indifference to all that concerns me and his own honour, these repeated and renewed proofs are too much for me ... If he goes to Bilgewater [the earl of Bridgewater at Ashridge] first I'll not receive him here'.[4]

Wyatt restored the cathedrals at Lichfield, Hereford and Durham as well as that in Salisbury. Some of this work involved essential repairs, such as the partial rebuilding of spires, or the addition of buttresses to the transept at Lichfield. At Hereford he was involved as a result of the collapse of a Norman tower and the partial destruction of the nave. Generally the aim of Wyatt's restorations, and of the Bishop and Cathedral Chapters that employed him, was also to *improve* the building by opening up vistas and creating large plain spaces rather than much smaller highly decorative ones. He was criticised for this approach and accused of not showing respect for the historical heritage in the buildings, yet his work reflected the fashions of the age and Prince Puckler-Muskau wrote of his work at Salisbury:

> The interior of this magnificent temple is in the highest degree inspiring and has been improved by Wyatt's genius. It was an admirable idea to remove the most remarkable old monuments from the walls and obscure corners and place them in the space between the great double avenue of pillars ... Nothing can have a finer effect.[5]

The work Wyatt did at Salisbury was preceded by earlier restoration campaigns. The bell tower had been damaged during the Civil War and it had not been repaired. Its removal had been approved in 1758, the timber spire was dismantled, and four years later some of the bells were sold though the bell tower survived at that stage.[6]

A programme of work was sponsored by Bishop John Hume (bishop 1766-82) and supervised by the cathedral surveyor Edmund Lush. The cathedral was closed for nearly two years from 1777 and the work involved removing the nave pulpit and pews, making new pews and galleries behind the choir stalls. The Presbytery was also extended into the Trinity Chapel and heating braziers were installed. The major donor was Lord Radnor and the 15th century Hungerford iron chantry chapel was moved from the north to the south side of the chancel and converted into the Radnor Pew.[7]

Shute Barrington (1734-1826) succeeded John Hume as bishop in 1782 and he incorporated the south-east corner of the churchyard into his garden. In

1786 Wyatt produced a measured plan of the Close, and set about levelling and draining the ground, removing the tombstones and covering over the ditches to create much of the open space that we see today.

In 1787 the Dean and Chapter asked Wyatt to survey the cathedral and the work that he suggested was approved on 26 August 1789. The driving force behind the changes seems to have been the bishop, Shute Barrington who had been at Salisbury since 1782. The cathedral was closed on 1 October 1789 and remained closed for three years while improvements were introduced – 'tidying up of the cathedral and the removal of clutter'.[8]

The biggest structural changes involved removal of the chantry chapels and stripping out everything between the choir and the Trinity Chapel, including a reredos behind the altar. The objective was to open out the eastern end and create a much-enlarged space within which the liturgy could take place.

It was claimed that the Hungerford and Beauchamp chapels were 'very dilapidated and [in an] unsafe condition'.[9] They had been defaced by the Puritans and were not used, though the antiquarian John Carter disputed this. In any event sale of the materials produced much needed revenue and Wyatt used parts of the buildings in creating a new pulpitum that would mark the division between the nave and the choir. The tombs that littered the eastern end were also removed and placed in neat lines between the nave columns.

Wyatt had planned to remove the original pulpitum to create an open vista. However the Bishop had already convinced George III that he should donate a new organ, and Wyatt was forced to abandon his original idea and to design a new pulpitum of stone that was robust enough to hold the organ above, even though this obscured the view down the cathedral in much the same way that the original screen had.[10]

In addition the stalls were cleaned, varnished and renovated and new canopies fitted, a new pulpit and Bishop's throne were installed, along with a communion rail, wainscot screens across the aisles and new paving, some of which was to be cut from old gravestones.

More controversially Wyatt planned to obliterate the coloured decoration on the walls and vault and to whitewash the interior. There was much objection and a set of drawings was produced of the decoration prior to its obliteration. These drawings would resurface three quarters of a century later when G G Scott attempted to undo most of what Wyatt had done.

The St Thomas porch on the north, and that dedicated to St Stephen on the south, were also taken down because they had not been built at the same time as the cathedral, a south door near the verger's house was blocked up and a new door opened up in the transept.[11]

Clearly the Dean and Chapter were having difficulties funding the building works. In 1791-2 the lead from the roof of the cloisters was removed and sold and slates used as a replacement. In 1792-3 a brass eagle and two spare bells were sold. In 1787 the Chapter had asked for an estimated value of the materials in the bell tower and in 1790 it was demolished. Over a lengthy period much of the stained glass was also removed so that the lead could be sold, though there is some doubt about whether Wyatt was party to this process.

Subsequently Wyatt was castigated for his changes and referred to as "Wyatt the Destroyer". As Richard Durman has demonstrated such criticism is perhaps a little unjustified as he was clearly working to the instructions of the Bishop, Dean and Chapter, and was also applying criteria that were seen as being acceptable by many at that time. In many ways he was a product of his age.[12]

However, within just 70 years the pendulum of taste had swung and G G Scott was employed to undo within the cathedral much of the effect that Wyatt had created.

George Gilbert Scott (1811-78) was appointed the architect of Salisbury cathedral in 1858.[13] He succeeded Henry Clutton who had converted to Roman Catholicism in 1856. One of Scott's first tasks was to complete the work Clutton had started restoring the Chapter House. He was also asked to survey the cathedral and report upon its condition.

Over the next 20 years Scott 'went about repairing the Cathedral and recreating a Gothic interior, sweeping away all traces of Wyatt's work.'[14] Scott was one of the most highly respected and prolific of the Victorian architects. He was responsible for creating the Albert Memorial in Kensington, the Midland Hotel at St Pancras, the Foreign Office building in Whitehall, Kelham Hall in Nottinghamshire for John Henry Manners-Sutton, Walton Hall in Warwickshire for Sir Charles Mordaunt, the chapel at Exeter College in Oxford plus hundreds of churches. In addition, he worked on the cathedrals at Bangor, Canterbury, Chester, Chichester, Durham, Ely, Exeter, Gloucester, Hereford, Lichfield, Peterborough, Ripon, Rochester, St Albans, St Asaph, St David's, Westminster and Worcester as well as that in Salisbury. This was a man at the top of his game.

Scott's survey report outlined a comprehensive programme of restoration and reordering. In 1862 the initial priority was to restore the exterior fabric, especially the troublesome tower and spire. Work on the west front followed in 1866-9. Then attention shifted to the interior, with the choir and chancel receiving much attention from 1869, along with the Trinity Chapel and eastern arm. This was mostly complete by 1875 when work started on the transepts and crossing, and then the nave from 1877. Scott was knighted in 1872. He died in 1878 and was succeeded by George Edmund Street.[15]

The external works, which started in 1862, included underpinning or repairing the foundations where this was needed and replacing damaged stonework in the external fabric, though the greatest attention was devoted to stabilising the tower.

The original cathedral was topped by a tower, against which the roofs of the nave, transepts and eastern end abutted.[16] Scott recounted how this

> Very light structure was intended to be visible from within. It is perforated in its thickness by a triforium gallery, leaving externally a wall of little more than two feet in thickness, while the inner consists of a light arcade with Purbeck marble shafts. The corner turrets have each a staircase, rendering them mere shells.

> On this frail structure the fourteenth-century builders carried up the vast tower, some eighty feet high, with walls nearly six feet thick, and upon this a spire rising 180 feet more. It need not then be wondered that the older storey, so unduly loaded, should have become shattered. Subsequent builders have bolstered it up by flying buttresses, and by every form of prop that they could invent, till, as Price calculated, the sectional area of the added supports exceed that of the original structure. Still, however, the crushing went on, and when I examined it, it had proceeded to very alarming lengths.[17]

The solution was to commission Francis Sheilds (see below from page 32) to insert four great iron scissor beams that pulled the four corners inwards and to then replace all the shattered and defective stonework in the walls. The ironwork is also strapped around the exterior of the four stair turrets and connected externally by vertical irons. Replacing the defective stone was a time consuming job as only small sections of stone were disturbed at any time, therefore maintaining maximum stability. By the time the work was completed Scott believed that 'the work was stronger than it had been when new'.[18]

The main columns in the crossing also attracted much attention because they were bent. Scott concluded that this was partly caused by the excessive weight coming from above, but also because only one side of each column was faced with Purbeck marble, while the other face was of 'compressible rubble walling'.[19] Scott recommended that a careful watch be maintained on the columns and action taken if the flexing continued.

Prior to starting the restoration work at Salisbury, Scott had been appointed to oversee the work of rebuilding the tower and spire at Chichester Cathedral. During a restoration of the cathedral there the columns supporting the tower and spire were seen to be in a poor structural state and the whole collapsed during a storm on 21 February 1861. Scott was called in to supervise the rebuilding and almost immediately became involved with a restoration of the tower and spire at Salisbury. It would have been unnatural if he had not taken steps to ensure that Salisbury never suffered the same fate as its sister cathedral at Chichester.

Having dealt with the general structure Scott's attention turned to the western

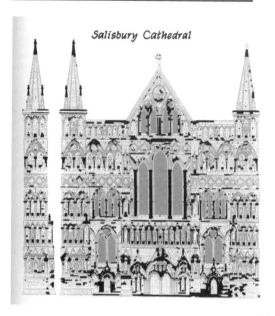

Salisbury Cathedral

The west front as restored by Scott. The stonework replaced by Scott is highlighted in black. Tim Ayres (ed), *Salisbury Cathedral: The West Front*, p97.

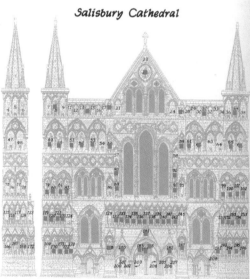

Salisbury Cathedral

The west front as restored by Scott. The statues replaced by Scott are highlighted in red. Adapted from Tim Ayres (ed), *Salisbury Cathedral: The West Front*, p97.

front in 1868. This western facade is more decorative and symbolic than structural and has been criticised in the past because it 'hid, rather than emphasised, the structure of the building'.[20] Its real purpose is to state in sculptural form the beliefs that led to the cathedral's construction, and that underlay the liturgy conducted there. The statues are organised in what C R Cockerell described as 'a *Te Deum* or theological scheme',[21] a *Te Deum Laudamus*.[22] Christ in majesty is at the top in the gable with a row of angels and archangels below. Then come Old Testament prophets, apostles, doctors, virgins and martyrs before close to the ground are worthies – bishops, princes and martyrs – especially those connected with Salisbury. The result is an arrangement of the whole body of the church assembled in praise of God above.

Scott was often accused of adopting an over enthusiastic approach to restoration work, though the evidence from his Salisbury work tends to question this assessment. Those involved with the recent restoration of the west end concluding that his work 'has proved to be remarkably conservative in extent and nature';[23] the work mainly 'consists of the addition or replacement of consoles for figure sculptures, capitals and shafts, together with restricted repairs to string-courses and arches'.[24]

However, the extent of the work is significant and best illustrated opposite. The upper highlights the masonry which was replaced or repaired by Scott while the lower shows the sculptures which were replaced or repaired. In total 56 new statues were erected and 15 medieval statues had new parts added (usually heads). The sculptural work was led by J F Redfern and the production rate saw seven or eight statues emerging every four months.

Having given initial attention to the exterior of the building, in 1869 the priority changed, with the choir becoming the major focus of attention. In the previous centuries a series of changes had been undertaken in the choir and chancel area that had altered the medieval arrangement. Scott's task was to return it to something like the original arrangement – 'to recreate a Gothic interior, as accurate as liturgical convenience would allow'.[25]

The diary of Francis Kilvert provides some insight into the state of the cathedral. His diary entry for Saturday 11 July 1874 records that:

> ' ...The Cathedral doors were open and I went in. One's first impression I think is of great size, roominess, airiness and lightness for the western doors were open, the townspeople were passing to and fro across the lawns of the Close in the sunshine and one seemed almost to be out of doors. The Choir is under restoration and will be very grand. The nave has not yet been touched and looks poor, bare, dirty and neglected. The town of Salisbury is wretched and dismal'.[26]

In the 13th century a pulpitum had marked the entrance to the choir and part of this remains in the west wall of the north-east transept. At the end of the 18th century Wyatt removed the medieval pulpitum and inserted a new screen that was intended to open up the view through the cathedral. Scott planned to replace this with a double screen that was supported on marble columns and topped with the organ.[27] However, the donor objected to the cost and an alternative iron design was produced by Francis Skidmore of Coventry for £1,000.[28]

There was much debate during the 19th century about the purpose of such

The Farmer & Brindley reredos which was removed in the 1960s.

screens. They marked the division between the congregational and clerical space, and marked off that part of the cathedral in which the main liturgical acts took place. Some argued that the congregation should only have an obscured view to emphasise the different areas, while others argued for openness and a more inclusive atmosphere. Scott's new design certainly provided the latter, and allowed the worshippers in the nave to see into the choir and so feel part of the liturgy.

Within the choir Scott set about restoring the choir stalls, stripping them of paint and generally restoring what existed. He also added new desks.[29] What exists today is a mix of medieval and 19th century woodwork but all arranged in a recreation of what was thought to have been the medieval pattern. In the process the side entrances into the choir from the choir aisles were reinstated and several tombs were uncovered.

In 1877 two new pulpits were created by Farmer & Brindley, one for inside the choir and another outside the screen. The latter still exists. It is built of Chilmark and Purbeck stone and is surrounded by statues of Noah, Elijah, Jonah and St John the Baptist. Francis Skidmore of Coventry produced the balustrade. The choir pulpit was replaced in 1961.

The gigantic Bishop's throne was also erected in 1877. It cost £590 and was

Scott's screen at Worcester Cathedral, made by Skidmore of Birmingham, which still remains.

made by Thomas Earp. The choir floor was relaid with encaustic tiles, though these have since been replaced with marble.[30]

To focus attention onto the altar, a giant reredos was erected behind the high altar. This was created by Farmer & Brindley, cost £1,800 and was the gift of Earl Beauchamp as a memorial of Bishop Beauchamp. The central focus was a crucifixion scene that very clearly linked what happened on the altar with Christ's sacrificial crucifixion. The reredos was removed in the 1960s.

Attempts were also made to recover some of the painted decoration on the vault. This had faded with time and been whitewashed over by Wyatt. Some pre-whitewash drawings existed and Clayton & Bell were commissioned to recreate the medieval images in the Trinity chapel, chancel and choir. Scott was ill when work on the Trinity chapel was undertaken and he expressed some disquiet when he returned. He was also far from happy with the decoration that was applied in the chancel and choir as the depictions were not completely accurate replications of the earlier decoration and Clayton & Bell had used their imagination where things were unclear. This was not the approach that a medieval seeking Goth, like Scott, approved of.

Finally Scott restored the memorial to Bishop Bingham (Bishop 1228/9-46, died 1246) that is located on the north side of the chancel, though apparently

The Farmer & Brindley reredos at Worcester which still survives and was similar to that in Salisbury.

he thought that it was the memorial to Bishop Richard Poore (Bishop 1217-28, died 1237). He then designed a memorial to Bishop Walter Kerr Hamilton (Bishop 1854-69, died 1869) in much the same style, and this was placed on the south side of the chancel and adjacent to the Radnor pew. This commemorated Bishop Hamilton in whose memory the reordering of the choir and chancel had been undertaken.[31]

By 1875 work on the chancel and choir was well underway and attention turned to restoring the transepts and crossing and then in 1877 work started on the nave. Scott died the following year and it fell to his successor, George Edmund Street, to complete the restoration work.[32]

Scott's work at Salisbury re-emphasised the Gothic and attempted to sweep away many of the 18th century changes, and especially those made by Wyatt. The aim was to recreate something closer to the original medieval ethos. Scott also stabilised and repaired the structure and prepared it for the 20th century. His work in the tower is particularly impressive and has made sure that the threat of collapse, so evident in Chichester, could not happen in Salisbury. However, fashions change with time and in the 1950s and 60s part of what Scott had done was changed and *The Friends of Salisbury Cathedral Thirty-First Annual Report* rejoiced at the removal of 'the distracting fussiness of the choir screen, the reredos, the encaustic tiles ...'.[33]

What Scott did at Salisbury he also did at a number of other cathedrals, and at Worcester much of this survives. There you will see an iron screen that was much the same in design as that installed at Salisbury and a spectacular reredos, plus the usual nave pulpit, vault decoration and Victorian floor tiles. There was talk of removing these additions in the 1960s but they survived as examples of the Victorian medieval dream.

John Elliott is an architectural historian who used to teach at the University of Reading and the University of London: Royal Holloway and Bedford New College. He is now retired and lives near Salisbury.

Bibliography

Alexander, B (ed), 1957, *Life at Fonthill, 1807–1822 with Interludes in Paris and London, from the Correspondence of William Beckford*, Rupert Hart-Davis

Ayres, Tim (ed), 2000, *Salisbury Cathedral: The West Front*, Phillimore

Brown, Sarah, 1999, *Sumptuous and Richly Adorn'd: The Decoration of Salisbury Cathedral*, Royal Commission on the Historical Monuments of England

Cocke, Thomas & Kidson, Peter, 1993, *Salisbury Cathedral: Perspectives on the Architectural History*, Royal Commission on the Historical Monuments of England

Dale, Anthony, 1936, *James Wyatt Architect 1746-1813*, Blackwell

Durman, Richard, 1997, James Wyatt and Salisbury Cathedral: The Demonising of an Architect, *Hatcher Review*, vol 5, no 43, (Spring)

Garlick, K, Macintyre, A, Cave, K & Newby, E (eds), 1978-98, *The diary of Joseph Farington*, Yale University Press, 17 vols

Plomer, William (ed), 1960, *Kilvert's Diary: 1870-1879: Life in the English Countryside in Mid-Victorian Times*, Jonathan Cape

Puckler-Muskau, *Tours in England*, 1832, Effingham Wilson, Royal Exchange

Stamp, Gavin (ed), 1995, Sir George Gilbert Scott, *Personal and Professional Recollections*, Paul Watkins

Tatton-Brown, Tim & Crook, John, 2009, *Salisbury Cathedral: The Making of a Medieval Masterpiece*, Scala

Notes

1   2667/20/22/3-11, 25 Jan 1775. Wardour MSS, Wiltshire and Swindon History Centre

2   Built as a set of winter assembly rooms, the Pantheon was later converted into a theatre, became a wine and spirit merchants and was demolished in 1937. Marks and Spencer's 'Oxford Street Pantheon' branch, at 173 Oxford Street now occupies the site

3   Garlick, Macintyre, Cave, & Newby, vol 9, p3465

4   Alexander, p129

5   Brown, p46 citing from Puckler-Muskau, vol 2, pp226–7. Prince Hermann Puckler-Muskau (1785-1871) was a German writer, traveller and garden designer. He toured English gardens in 1816 and then began work on making a landscape park at Muskau which turned out to be too expensive. He sold the estate and used the proceeds to buy a smaller one at Schloss Branitz near Kottbus. His garden work is supposed to show the influence of Lancelot Brown and Humphry Repton

6   Dale, p48 cites the Chapter Acts Book 1758

7   See Tatton–Brown, p119

8   Tatton–Brown, p121

9   Durman, p45

10 See Tatton–Brown, p121. Richard Durman says that William Dodsworth, a cathedral verger, claimed the original pulpitum was removed by Wyatt because it was 'so judiciously situated as to hide the lower part of the pillars' (Durman, p47)

11 For more details see Dale, pp44-5

12 See Durman.

13 In his recollections he says that he was appointed 'I think, about 1859' (see Stamp p300), though in his unpublished notebooks he says 'I think I was appointed in 1858' (see Stamp p479)

14 Brown p47

15 For a summarised chronology see Tatton-Brown & Crook, p124

16 This tower is now located above the vault of the crossing and contains the clock mechanism that drives the bells. The original vault on top of this tower was removed and the new tower built on top.

17 Stamp, p301-2

18 Stamp, p303

19 *Ibid*

20 Ayres, p107

21 *Builder* 15 May 1869, p384

22 An early Christian hymn of praise with the title taken from the opening Latin words, *Te Deum laudamus*, meaning 'Thee, O God, we praise'

23 Ayres, p94

24 Ayres, p95

25 See Brown, p48

26 Plomer, Volume 3 page 49

27 Some of Skidmore's screen still exists. Part is in the Victoria & Albert Museum, part is in the cathedral cloister and part is in the altar rail in Alderbury church

28 See Brown pp48 & 99

29 The desks were the flat sections used to support the service books. The canopies were added in 1913

30 See Brown, p49

31 See Brown, p48

32 Street worked on the north porch, making gates for the choir aisle entrances and the organ case (1877)

33 *The Friends of Salisbury Cathedral Thirty-First Annual Report* (May 1961), pp27–8

F W Wentworth Sheilds 1820– 1906. The Engineer who saved Salisbury's Spire

David Richards

When Salisbury Cathedral was consecrated in 1258 it looked significantly different from the building seen today. The finished tower barely rose above the roofline and was probably topped by a relatively low wooden lantern or spire[1]. A generation later an extraordinarily bold decision was taken to build two additional storeys onto the tower to support a stone spire and create a structure 404 feet (123 metres) high. This additional 6,300 tons[2] of masonry put the original tower under enormous stress. Despite the immediate insertion of stone buttressing and wrought iron supports the new masonry started to distort the old. Examination today of the pillars of the tower at the crossing inside the Cathedral clearly shows how solid stone has been caused to visibly bend. Repeated attempts over the centuries were made to stop the advance of this but by the time George Gilbert Scott was appointed as the Cathedral architect[3] in the 1850s the situation was causing considerable concern.

Scott says in his book 'The tower was crushed in the most frightful way imaginable'[4]. At a public meeting in the Chapter House of Salisbury Cathedral the Dean repeated Scott's words, warning of 'failure at any moment'[5]. Scott's plan was to stabilise and support it with diagonal iron ties and then repair the stonework. However, it appears that the Dean and Chapter were not entirely convinced as Scott then writes 'the Chapter for further consideration called in the aid of an engineer eminent for iron construction, Mr Sheilds, whose opinion very much coincided with my own. To him was confided the arrangement and construction of the iron–work, which was admirably carried out under his direction by Messrs James of London'[6]. These internal wrought iron beams are monolithic and massively strong; an impressive and confident example of mid–

A view of Sheilds' wrought iron beams from above. Note how individual beams split to encircle the corners of the tower and the enclosed staircases. Above the 19th century beams are the thinner 14th century iron ties.

Victorian engineering. The beams join diagonally opposite corners of the tower on four separate levels. Each of them today is still covered with canvas that holds a layer of horse hair in contact with the iron, an arrangement probably designed to minimise the effects of condensation. Externally, on the base of the tower, the beams are clearly and visibly fixed with vertical and horizontal strips of iron. Scott may have influenced Sheilds to over–engineer the ironwork following the collapse of the spire of Chichester Cathedral in 1861[7]. Scott had been the architect commissioned to rebuild the shattered tower and spire in Chichester and his fear of a similar collapse at Salisbury would have been at the forefront of his mind. On its completion Scott said 'It is a very fine engineering work'[8]

Salisbury Cathedral was suddenly national news. Public meetings, chapter meetings and fundraising in Salisbury were reported in a series of articles and letters in *The Times*. In early August 1865 it was reported in *The Times* that Chapter approved the tower plans. Almost immediately an anonymous letter to the Editor was published alleging that the iron work was ugly and unsafe[9]. A few days later F W Sheilds replied 'as the engineer who designed the ironwork in question' and corrected this untruth. An article appeared in *The Times* on 14

Wrought Iron

There are three basic forms of iron: cast, wrought, and steel.

Cast Iron is made by pouring molten pig iron, obtained by refining iron ore, into moulds. It contains a high amount of carbon (between 2% and 4%) and solidifies to be hard and relatively brittle.

Wrought iron is made from pig iron or 'bloom' and contains very little carbon (approximately 0.035%) and is malleable with a high tensile strength. The word 'wrought' indicates the iron has been worked on by heating and hammering (or rolling). Note also the difference between medieval and 19th century wrought iron. Until the 19th century, wrought iron was made in intimate contact with the charcoal of the fire. This metal is now referred to as 'charcoal iron' to differentiate it from the later 'puddled iron' made in coal heated reverberatory furnaces.

Mild steel is the modern replacement[12] of wrought iron containing a moderate amount of carbon (between 0.06% and 2%) that corrodes easily.

From the 14th to the 19th centuries wrought iron was a vital element in the efforts to maintain the physical integrity of Salisbury Cathedral tower and to prevent its possible structural failure. Its unique qualities of hardness, tensile strength, ductility and durability contained within a relatively small mass made it an ideal building support. Unfortunately, in a pre—industrial society the mining and refining of iron ore with large quantities of charcoal was an expensive process. Despite this, extensive iron supports were inserted into Salisbury Cathedral's tower, from the 14th century onwards on a total of nine separate occasions, including a scheme by Christopher Wren, before Sheilds' version.[13] It is interesting to note that the vast wooden roof of the cathedral was originally constructed largely without the use of iron nails. Iron was only used in buildings during the medieval period when there was no alternative.

The economics of iron production had changed dramatically when Sheilds designed his iron supports. The advent of steam power in all its forms ensured that wrought iron produced in coal fired puddle furnaces became an everyday material. It is no coincidence that at about this time Salisbury saw a large, secular building arise in the centre of the city, the Market House, with its roof, gates and internal galleries and supporting pillars being largely constructed of iron.

Today, the medieval and Victorian iron in the tower remains as a fascinating industrial archaeological source that attracts numerous academic and general visitors.

F W Wentworth Sheilds

Close up of the joint between sections of Sheilds' beams showing how they are retained by wedges and not by bolts.

August 1866 saying the work had been completed to the entire satisfaction of Scott and Sheilds. Another dated 30 April 1875 gave the cost of tower repairs as £4138 4s 4d.

So who was this Mr Sheilds? His obituary[10] records that Francis Webb Wentworth Sheilds was an Irishman born in 1820. His father was the Rev Wentworth Sheilds, Rector of Kilbeg in County Meath. Steam locomotives developed rapidly during the early decades of the 19th century and influenced Sheilds' decision to become a railway engineer and surveyor. He received his early training from Charles Vignoles (1793–1875), Past–President of the Institute of Civil Engineers[11] and a leading Irish railway engineer.

In 1843 Sheilds sailed to Australia and obtained the post of engineer to the city of Sydney. A few years later the Sydney Railway Company was formed to build one of the first railways in Australia, between Sydney and its western suburb of Parramatta[14], a distance of 14 miles. Sheilds was appointed the chief engineer. He was to champion the broad gauge instead of standard gauge and start a conflict of engineering views that was to bedevil Australian railways until modern times. Unfortunately the company ran out of money and reduced his salary from £400 to £300. Sheilds was unhappy with this, resigned and returned to England. Interestingly, he was to renew his connections with Australia as

External iron fixings for the four levels of internal beams. Note near the top of the image the lead covering the external 14th century wrought iron ties.

Inspecting Engineer to the New South Wales Government between 1873 and 1875.

In 1852 he became a resident engineer in Sydenham for the re–building of the Crystal Palace[15], a job he held till 1858. This association led to a commission from the Portuguese to design and build a version of the Crystal Palace in Oporto. This was opened by the King and Queen of Portugal in 1861[16]. Sadly, like its British inspiration, it has now disappeared without trace. Using his long experience with iron, Sheilds wrote in 1861 what was to become a Victorian engineering classic *The Strains on Structures of Ironwork*. This book together with his Crystal Palace work may have brought him to the attention of G G Scott. Sheilds worked with Scott on the Albert Memorial foundations and internal ironwork for the flèche,[17] Shakespeare's Stratford on Avon church as well as Salisbury Cathedral.

In 1861 the Thames Embankment Commission was set up to hold a competition for designing an embankment from Westminster to Blackfriars on the Thames in London and Sheilds was singled out as one the best of the 50 entries. Unfortunately for Sheilds, another engineer got the job, prompting him to take his case for unpaid expenses to parliament. Despite widespread publicity through the national press, he lost.[18] The government asked him to design a cross channel bridge but he decided it was impractical. The government also asked his opinion (and took it) on the building of the new law courts in the Strand designed by G E Street. When Scott died in 1878 Street became Salisbury Cathedral's architect.

During his professional lifetime Sheilds worked with Scott as well as building many railways bridges, docks and sewage works in England and overseas. He retired to Southampton and built the sewage works at Bitterne and Woolston, the last job he ever did. He died in 1906 and is buried in Southampton. One of his sons became an Australian Bishop and another a distinguished civil engineer[19] involved in the building of the new Southampton docks. Admirers of the gothic glory of Salisbury Cathedral Spire should note that it was Scott's structural survey of the tower that predicted its imminent disintegration. Sheilds' work prevented this. In 1987 Peter Taylor, the then consultant engineer to Salisbury Cathedral, wrote 'Sheilds, advising Scott in the 19th century, designed a set of iron ties ... there is little doubt that this is the best of the strengthening devices added to the structure up to that time, and it continues to serve its purpose well.'[20] It is fitting that Sheilds should be remembered as the former railway engineer who saved the tower and spire of Salisbury Cathedral from catastrophic collapse.

David Richards is a retired dental surgeon who is now a Blue Badge guide with a particular interest in the history of the people and buildings of the Salisbury area.

Bibliography

Cocke, T & Kidson, P, 1993, *Salisbury Cathedral,* RCHM

Scott, G G, 1995, *Personal and Professional Recollections*, Paul Watkins

Photographs by the author

Notes

1 Simpson, G & Miles, D, 2005, Salisbury Cathedral's Tower and Spire, *Sarum Chronicle,* issue 5, pp3–9
2 Cocke, & Kidson, p11
3 George Gilbert Scott RA (1810–1878) was Cathedral architect from 1858 to 1878
4 Scott, p479
5 *The Times*, 9 April 1864, p12
6 Scott, p302
7 Elliott, John P, 1995, *The Architectural Works of Richard Cromwell Carpenter (1812–55), William Slater (1819–72) & Richard Herbert Carpenter (1841–93)*, unpublished PhD thesis, University of London.
8 Scott, p479
9 *The Times*, 29 August 1865, p9
10 *Journal of the Institute of Civil Engineers*, 1906, volume CLXVIII, p353
11 Sheilds was elected an Associate of the Institute of Civil Engineers in 1856 and a Member in 1859.
12 Henry Bessemer demonstrated a modern method of steel production with the Bessemer process in 1856 and opened the Bessemer Steel Works in Sheffield in 1858. It took until the 1870s for the process to be widely accepted and adopted by significant numbers of other steel companies. This was just a little too late for Sheilds to use the new mild steel at Salisbury.
13 Cocke, & Kidson, p10, fig 2
14 *Bulletin* (Australia Railway Historical Society),1999, vol 50, no 744, Oct, pp367–384
15 The Crystal Palace had previously hosted the Great Exhibition of 1851 in London's Kensington Gardens
16 *Illustrated London News,* 18 November 1865
17 Brooks, C (ed), 2000, *The Albert Memorial*, Yale University Press, pp137–38
18 *The Times*, 21 December 1864, p7
19 His son Wentworth Francis Wentworth–Sheilds became Bishop of Armidale in Australia. His son Frank Wentworth Sheilds was a distinguished engineer responsible for the reclamation of 400 acres of waterside land in Southampton and the design of the huge George V dry dock in Southampton.
20 Taylor, Peter, 1987, The Tower & Spire of Salisbury Cathedral, *Association for the Study of the Conservation of Historic Buildings Transaction*, Volume 12, p7

Laverstock House Asylum: A kindly tradition, 200 years of mental health care

Ruth Newman

Salisbury held a unique position in the care of the mentally ill. Two private asylums, Laverstock House and Fisherton Asylum (later the Old Manor hospital), meant that there were more psychiatric patients here than anywhere in the country outside London. Despite some conflicting evidence they seem generally to have been progressive and well run, contradicting the stereotypical views of such early 19th century institutions with purging, blood letting and physical restraint. Not as well known nationally as the Quaker foundation, the *Retreat*, at York, in many ways Laverstock House set in its 12 acres of grounds, emulates and predates its more famous contemporary. William Tuke at the *Retreat* in the late 18th century developed the concept of 'moral management' (treatment through kindness and reason), already in practice at Laverstock. The madness of George III brought a growing awareness of mental health treatment and attitudes began to change. The Victorian asylum movement was visionary in its utopian ideals with a growing belief in non–restraint and by 1850 it was generally accepted that lunatics were best treated in certified, protected 'asylums' – places of security and shelter.

Many Georgian provincial madhouse keepers founded family businesses which survived for several generations. Salisbury's asylums, just outside the city boundary, were established and run by members of the Finch family who also owned a further unidentified Wiltshire house and two others in London. The early history of Laverstock House is uncertain. Often described as a private 'mad house' since the mid 18th century,[1] it was certainly between 1770–1772 a centre where patients could be inoculated against smallpox. By December 1770 it had opened 'for the reception of patients in inoculation by Daniel Sutton & Co'. A

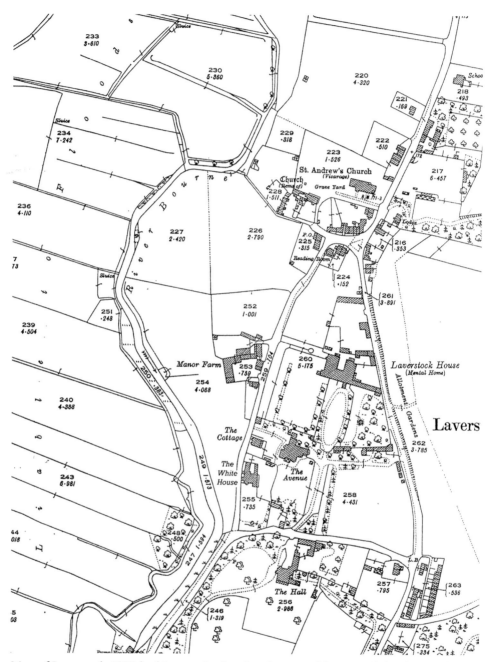

Map of Laverstock 1925 looking north, showing the mental home and the doctors' houses within the asylum triangle

Laverstock from the air looking south, showing the old asylum triangle bordered by Duck Lane, The Avenue and Riverside Road, photograph by Joe Newman, 2008

later advert stresses 'the excellency of the Sutton method of inoculation, as more than ninety thousand have been inoculated without the loss of a single patient.[2]

The period from the 1770s until the mid 19th century saw a rapid expansion in provincial mad houses. Unease about the condition in which lunatics were kept led to the Lunacy Act of 1774 where private houses had to be licensed and inspected regularly with the number of patients recorded. Originally there were three categories of patients: private patients, disruptive paupers from the workhouses where payment was made by the parish of legal settlement, and criminal lunatics, guilty but insane and paid for by the Home Office. Laverstock never received the last category but Fisherton Asylum took considerable numbers only declining after 1863 with the opening of the specialist Broadmoor Hospital.

Laverstock House was sold by auction in April 1777[3] and was probably purchased in 1779 by William Finch who practiced at Milford; nearly 180 years later, in 1955, Laverstock House Nursing Home for Nervous and Mental Disorders, closed. Finch was the founder of a dynasty of asylum owners, and although a non–medical proprietor he was practical enough to claim in the earliest surviving advert of 1779, 'great success in curing people disordered in their senses' asserting that every person 'he has had charge of ... has been cured and discharged perfectly well'.[4]

An advert in the *Salisbury Journal* of 1784 is one of many promoting the asylum. 'William Finch ... has removed to Laverstock House where he receives ... lunatic patients. The House is delightfully situated on an eminence about one mile from Salisbury, opening into a beautiful extensive garden with every other accommodation for ... any lady or gentleman needing such a retreat'.[5] Kindness was the watchword rather than restraint and he was described on his death as a man 'much respected for integrity and humanity'.[6] Two of his 14 children, William and Charles, became doctors. Laverstock House passed first to his son, Dr William Finch (1776–1848), who later in 1813 established Fisherton Asylum. Dr Finch quickly stressed his medical credentials and the continuity of the establishment, his mother, Caroline in charge of the 'domestic part of the house' whilst he had been 'bred up under his Father in the business' with a 'liberal and medical education'.[7] Mrs Caroline Finch sought to attract more females: 'Mrs Finch, Widow of the late Mr William Finch ... proposes receiving at her NEW HOUSE, at Laverstock, FEMALE LUNATICS ONLY, where the mode of treatment of those unhappily afflicted with mental derangement ... will be calculated to afford the best possible relief and comfort to her patients'. This appears to be in a separate building within the grounds.[8]

There is no evidence to confirm the first William Finch's success in curing all his patients. It seems at the very least an exaggeration when looking at later statistics. A register of patients for Laverstock is available from 1797 to 1955. Whilst not a complete record in the early years, it remains a valuable source on the patients admitted, the length of stay, and condition when they left. Many recorded patients, certainly initially, were long term. The second person in the register in 1797 was a 40 year old Frenchman, M Darins. He was committed by

Copy

Statement and Order to be annexed to the Medical Certificates, authorising the Reception of an Insane Person.

The Patient's true Christian and Surname at full length .... *Susan Bullar*

The Patient's Age .... *23 years*

Married or Single .... *single*

The Patient's previous Occupation (if any) ....

The Patient's previous place of abode .... *Fletchwood, Hants*

The licensed House, or other place (if any), in which the Patient was before confined ....

Whether found Lunatic by Inquisition, and date of Commission .... *no*

Special circumstance which shall prevent the Patient being separately examined by two Medical Practitioners .... *none*

Special circumstance which exists to prevent the insertion of any of the above particulars .... *none*

SIRS,

Upon the Authority of the above Statement, and the annexed Medical Certificates, I request you will receive the said *Miss Susan Bullar* as a Patient into your House. I am, Sirs, your obedient Servant,

(Signed) Name .... *Charles Maud*

Occupation (if any) .... *Surgeon*

Place of Abode .... *Southampton*

Degree of Relationship (if any) to the Insane Person .... *none*

To Dr. FINCH and Mr. LACY,
Proprietors of Laverstock House, Wilts.

FORM OF MEDICAL CERTIFICATES.

I, the undersigned, hereby certify, that I separately visited and personally examined *Miss Susan Bullar* the Person named in the annexed Statement and Order, on the *16* day of *October* one thousand eight hundred and thirty *four* and that the said *Miss Susan Bullar* is of unsound Mind, and a proper Person to be confined.

(Signed) Name .... *Joseph Bullar*

Physician, Surgeon, or Apothecary .. *M.D. Surgeon*

Place of Abode .... *5 High Street Southampton*

I, the undersigned, hereby certify, that I separately visited and personally examined *Miss Susan Bullar* the Person named in the annexed Statement and Order, on the *16* day of *October* one thousand eight hundred and thirty *four* and that the said *Miss Susan Bullar* is of unsound Mind, and a proper Person to be confined.

(Signed) Name .... *William Bullar*

Physician, Surgeon, or Apothecary .. *M.D. Surgeon*

Place of Abode .... *Southampton*

W. B. BRODIE AND CO., PRINTERS, SARUM.

Medical certificate, Susan Bullar 1834, WSA A1/563

the government, a 'foreigner', at the time of the French wars possibly regarded as a threat to national security. He died in the asylum, aged 73, in 1830.[9]

After the 1828 Madhouses Act, which improved inspection and regulation, new certificates were required, signed by two doctors which should have avoided possible collusion between the family and local doctor. Notwithstanding legal requirements the certificates of admission which give considerable detail on the patients, often raise unanswerable suspicions. Susan Bullar, aged 23, was placed in the House on 16 October, 1834 by a Charles Maud (surgeon and no relation) but the medical certificates were signed by Doctors Joseph and William Bullar. She was removed 'cured' on 5 November 1835. Just contemporary with Susan Bullar, the 18 year old Julia Saunders from the Isle of Wight was placed in the asylum by her father on 6 September 1834 and 'removed [by him] therefrom on the 20th day of October 1834. Cured', posing the question as to why a young girl was so confined for just six weeks.[10]

Occasional incidents come to light which were reported in the press. In 1816, one of the passengers in the Quicksilver mail coach failed to escape to the safety of the inn after the leading horse was attacked by a lioness at *The Winterslow Hut* (later *The Pheasant Inn*). He survived his confrontation to give a report to the newspapers, then collapsed and spent the next 27 years in Laverstock Asylum. 'He is now, Dr Finch thinks, an incurable patient.'[11] Some years later *The Times* reported that an aspiring suitor to the young Queen Victoria who 'conceives himself to be king of several countries' managed to elude the royal guard and 'gained access to the Palace'. A warrant was issued 'but as his insanity was manifest, and his connexions highly respectable ... he has been placed in the asylum of Dr Finch of Laverstock.'[12]

A fascinating account from the 1820s of the asylum has recently come to light; Thomas Campbell, the Scottish poet,[13] was faced in the early 1820s with the dilemma that his son, Thomas Telford Campbell, aged 18, was becoming increasingly disturbed. He looked for a 'temporary home' for his son, and discovered Laverstock Asylum 'and thither the afflicted parents had the painful task of conducting their only child.'[14] In a letter written by Campbell he states that 'their establishment speaks for itself; their kindness inspires unlimited confidence ... I have put him into Dr. F's hand, implicitly'. He found Dr and Mrs Finch 'zealously interested in the recovery of their patients ... Everything is open at all times to inspection.' Of the condition of his son; 'Dr F ... believed the taint to be of long standing, and that the cure ... might be stubborn.'[15] Campbell described a not altogether comfortable visit which he and his wife made to the asylum in October 1822. 'We came to a garden terrace ... A female [patient] dressed like a nun, was parading ... there was an air of quiescent madness in her gray eyes ... By and by, a poor man came out – a pauper patient – limping and hanging his pallid head ... we heard a dismal howling, but very soon discovered that ... Dr. F. keeps a pack of hounds for his patients to hunt with. But the momentary belief of its being the voice of human beings, made one's blood run cold. At last, we came in full sight of a beautiful house and spacious grounds ... the black man who opened the outward gate, I have since understood to be an excellent creature.'[16]

Rare grafted manna ash; garden of author, photograph by Joe Newman

They were met by Dr Finch and his wife, who did much to allay their fears. The Campbells spent the day at the asylum with their son, enjoyed dinner with the Finches and 'two very well–behaved patients' and took the coach back to London.[17]

Campbell was not completely satisfied with Laverstock asylum; 'I have had a letter from Dr Finch, giving a most ambiguous and vague account of Thomas's case ... there is a want of *special* observation in the report.' Thomas appears to have returned home after a year with 'little benefit [having] resulted from the experiment', but further difficulties saw the son's return in November 1824 but, he adds, 'the more I think of [the superiority] of Laverstock, the more mitigated I feel by my poor boy's misfortune'.[18]

An undated prospectus for 'Laverstock House Retreat' (probably 1824) stresses the improvements to the accommodation, facilities for the 'most compleat separation of *Male from Female patients'*. Apartments were also subdivided according to 'station in Life' with whole apartments for high fee–paying patients. The prospectus quotes the 1815–16 reports taken from the Select Commission on Madhouses, to whom Finch gave evidence. Laverstock was highly praised as one of the finest private asylums in existence. The Quaker, Edward Wakefield, visited the institution, reporting that he 'conducts his house in an admirable manner. He has 120 patients ... not a single patient in a strait jacket ... Every possible kind of amusement was provided for them; billiards, backgammon, cards, books etc in doors; bowls, cricket, greyhounds, riding on horseback and in a carriage, out of doors'. 'It appears to be his great object to keep the mind continually at work upon anything but that which engages it under disease'. He also noted that Dr Finch kept a book registering the 'peculiarities of the disease of every patient, and the mode of treatment which has been adopted' including the 'rotatory' chair which spun patients round causing vertigo and vomiting. This was described *'as most useful as the pain it excites takes the patients' minds on to it rather than the disease',* but generally, under the Finch family, there was a desire not to resort to mechanical devices or seclusion.[19]

The prospectus and indeed every advert stresses 'the absence of all coercion' adhering to the 'moral management' philosophy of the time. 'Sympathy', 'humanity' and 'kindness' were fashionable words in the treatment of mental illness in the early 19th century. Finch also stressed the 'careful selection of servants', the importance of advances in medical treatment and 'the improved practice of his medical friends'.[20] The need for early treatment was reinforced with impressive figures to endorse his preventative measures. 'Of every 100 patients admitted here, within three months from the first attack of insanity, there were cured 88 ... Of every 100 admitted whose insanity had been had been existing more than five years, there were cured only 12. The number of patients here under restraint does not exceed two and a half percent.[21]

Even before 1815 pleasure grounds were laid out at Laverstock to provide walks for the patients based on the idea of a country estate with nine acres for 'superior patients' and about one acre for paupers. From a mound within the asylum patients could see the road outside without being viewed themselves. Much attention was placed on the environment, designed to be both restful and therapeutic. Magnificent ornamental trees which date back to the first half of the 19th century still survive, including a rare grafted manna ash.

Following the 1828 Act asylums had to be visited four times a year and minutes kept. Under the Finch family the Visitors' reports generally portray a progressive, humane establishment. The 1829 report is typical: 'Having ... seen all the patients ... the visitors have satisfaction in stating that the apartments are particularly clean and well ventilated and the gardens and airing grounds spacious and well calculated for air and exercise and the accommodation in every respect proper for the number of patients. That every attention appears to have been paid to the health and comfort of the patients who are allowed much exercise and amusement as the nature of their cases permit'.[22] Visitors could set at liberty persons who they considered to be improperly confined.

A copy of the visitors' minutes of 7 May 1835 reported that they were 'satisfied of the insanity of the whole. Not a single doubtful case'.

Patients in the House	104	Under restraint – two women
Curable men	21	
Incurable men	37	
Curable women	21	
Incurable women	25[23]	

The October 1842 report further noted the generous patient/staff ratio; '128 patients attended by 18 men and 25 female servants ... Dr Finch has added two padded cells, one for male and one for female pauper patients'.[24]

Plans exist for both 1829 and 1844 following alterations to the asylum. The later general plan shows the 'buildings and premises', including the asylum within its landscaped grounds, the chapel, several cottages, an extensive cricket pitch and a large kitchen garden and drying area for laundry. The house opposite the main entrance was 'The Hall', the private residence of Dr Finch. The detailed plan of the asylum for 1844 includes the padded cells mentioned above, a brewhouse, granaries, the paupers' yards, 64 bedrooms and 19 privies/water closets.[25]

There needed to be a compromise between the families' concern for confidentiality and the demands of increased regulation after 1828. William Finch (the younger) realised the importance of good management as well as medicine. He complained that the Wiltshire magistrates threatened to withdraw his licence because he was unwilling to reveal the location of his ex–patients after discharge. The same 1828 act recommended that church services should be performed in asylums. The 'soothing effect of Religion' had been incorporated into life at Laverstock as early as 1815 [26] but from 1828–9 a purpose built chapel, 'a very neat and Commodious Building' was available in the grounds. 'Divine service is regularly performed by Mr Lacy ... for the benefit of the patients'. Others regularly attended St Andrew's Church in the village and were buried in the parish churchyard with just initials on their headstones. Whilst an increased emphasis was placed on the healing powers of religion the management was careful to exclude those suffering from religious delusions.[27]

There are few references to charges at Laverstock. In an early example of care in the community, Dr Finch concluded a printed handbill of 1807 by adding that 'patients are attended by Mr Finch, at their own houses; and careful and experienced servants sent in cases which will not admit a removal'.[28] This appears to be the case not just for the wealthy. Bills were sent to the churchwardens and overseers of the poor at Britford in 1808–9 for Jane Tinham, the wife of Joseph,

Laverstock Asylum within its extensive grounds, photograph c1900, WSA 3433/1/38

'a labourer and poor person'. She was 'so far disordered in her senses that it is dangerous for her ... to go abroad and that ... for her safety some proper person should be provided to take care of [her] during her lunacy'. This apparently was not sufficient because she was removed to Laverstock House. A bill for £12 3s for the year from Easter 1808 included board, medicine, visits and attendance on her at Britford. A later bill included payment of a 'servant to inform you of death', the costs of her coffin and 'laying out'.[29] A further charge to the overseers at Longbridge Deverill was for the 'Board, Lodging and mending etc of Benjamin Wheeler' from 14 August 1813 to 10 May 1814 at 14 shillings a week. The total costs were £29 10s, considerably more than maintaining pauper lunatics in the community and therefore they were only sent to asylums when unmanageable.[30]

The fees for private patients varied according to their wealth and status. An advert of 1814 refers to 'another suite of apartments ... for a limited number of Patients of the superior class' who could occasionally bring their servants.[31] A financial discussion with Dr Finch was recorded by Thomas Campbell over the admission of his son in 1822. Campbell wrote of the fees varying from two to ten guineas a week and suffered anxieties in wanting to do what was best, but 'could not afford to place him among the class of boarders who paid at the rate of five hundred a year ... I therefore told Dr F ... that although I should not mind for [up to] a year, to encounter pretty high terms, if he continued a long time, I should be obliged to place him on the lowest terms, since even on these, he would probably cost me £150 a year'.[32]

Laverstock House Asylum

Wiltshire was an important centre for pauper lunacy. Most came from outside the county, Laverstock taking considerable numbers of females from the Isle of Wight workhouses. After 1828 the state of mind of the pauper had to be recorded when removed; Sarah Sickman, placed in the asylum by the Andover overseers in January 1835 was removed 'cured' in June of the same year.[33] As a result Laverstock became one of the largest provincial licensed houses in the country with over 100 patients for the first 50 years of the 19th century, reaching a peak of 135 in 1841, but with provision for 50 paupers and 100 private patients. The 1847 'pauper dietary' appears generous by the standards of the time eg for dinner '½lb hot meat, beef or mutton with vegetables, 1½ pints of beer and on Sundays ¼lb suet pudding'. Women had the same as men 'but in rather less proportions' though with vast quantities of tea. The pauper men worked in the gardens and farm whilst the women worked in the kitchen and washhouse. Patients thus employed were 'allowed two extra pints of beer daily with snuff and tobacco and have their meals in the kitchen with the servants'.[34]

Under the terms of the 1845 Lunacy Act every county was required to build a pauper lunatic asylum and Laverstock's pauper intake ended when such patients were removed to Roundway Hospital in 1851, the county asylum at Devizes.

Grave of William Finch (1776–1848), Laverstock churchyard, photograph by Joe Newman

The census of that year showed 120 private patients, 61 male and 59 female.

A delightful report from the *Salisbury Journal* reveals how Dr Finch saw the asylum as part of the wider community in the post 1832 Reform celebrations. 'On Saturday last, the village of Laverstock ... was all life and gaiety, owing to an invitation ... by Dr Finch and Mr Lacy, to the inhabitants of the parish to an excellent supper ... Two hundred and ten sat down ... under an avenue of trees, in the outer grounds of the Asylum ... A band of music was in attendance, and after supper, dances were introduced, whilst the elders smoked their pipes, and the children diverted themselves on the green ... Gothic lanterns tastefully hung amongst the trees'.[35] Villagers for their part saw the 'House' as providing employment; in 1881 for just 43 patients, staff included Dr Manning as medical superintendent, a matron, three cooks, six nurses, four housemaids, four laundresses, four male hospital attendants and a gardener. Most of these came from Laverstock or nearby and this continued well into the 20th century. [36]

Dr Finch died in 1848 with the business passing to 'the superintendence' of his widow, Mrs Mary Finch, assisted by Dr J W Finch Noyes and Dr Hewson.[37] The involvement of the Finch family at Laverstock ended in 1854 following Mary's death but continued at Fisherton into the early 20th century. From the mid 19th century Laverstock was no longer at the forefront of mental health care, but the institution with 74 private patients remained one of the largest private, provincial licensed hospitals in the country. The pauper buildings were pulled down to provide suitable accommodation for the middle classes. The *Salisbury Journal* in 1855 referred to Laverstock House as being 'recently rebuilt at an outlay of many thousand pounds' and 'none but private patients admitted'.[38] A charming anonymous pamphlet, *'Our holiday in Laverstock Park asylum'* was published in 1860. Clearly promotional, it was produced when the institution was facing criticism. Dr Bushnan, the proprietor, invited 50 (Southampton) medical men to view his 'House' and the booklet described their visit. The patients were compared to 'happy school boys at play', enjoying bowls on billiard smooth lawns, or appreciating the well stocked library. The ladies had their own 'elegantly furnished sitting rooms' and flower gardens. There were outings to the Cathedral and Stonehenge, fly fishing 'in the neighbouring streams' and both diet and treatment were described in glowing terms, 'a model of the very best type of asylum for the insane'.[39]

Nationally, by the mid 19th century there was a widespread belief in moral management and non–restraint, but this was followed in the late 19th/early 20th centuries by the pessimistic belief that lunacy was innate, with a regression in attitudes and to an extent, this was reflected at Laverstock. A Commissioners' report of 1862 when there were 41 patients of each sex wrote that 'although under the present proprietor (Dr J S Bushnan) the general management ... has on

Laverstock House Asylum

Laverstock House Mental Hospital 1930s (photograph, private collection)

the whole been satisfactory' and 'arrangements for exercise are good' the visiting magistrates had frequently complained of a 'want of neatness' and 'personal cleanliness'. Even worse, seclusion and 'mechanical restraint [are] occasionally employed to a considerable extent'.

Three years later the house was in much worse condition; it had fallen into the hands of a 'non–medical proprietor who regards it as a money speculation only'. A patient had committed suicide and 'great dissatisfaction' of the medical officer was expressed. The justices brought pressure to bear on the house by renewing the licence for three months only during which time improvements were made. By 1867 Joseph Haynes was the owner while Dr S L Haynes and Dr Henry John Manning were listed as the joint medical superintendents and by the 1870s reports of the accommodation and care were very good.[40]

During this decade Julia Wood, aged 60, was placed in the asylum by her nephew. She became a benefactor to an obscure 'Children of God' religious sect, the New Forest Shakers, and was certified insane after offering £2000 to build them a lodge in the New Forest. Wood's nephew wrote out a lunacy order and went with doctors, police officers and a nurse from Laverstock to the Shaker camp. Julia resisted arrest but was taken by carriage to the asylum where she was said to be suffering from 'religious hallucinations'. Her entry in the Register states that she was admitted in February, 1875 and finally discharged in December, 1881 'not improved'. She spoke highly of her treatment under Dr Manning, the

Personal memories of Laverstock House

In the 20th century, the mental hospital appears to have been accepted with some affection in the village. In the 1940s and 1950s villagers 'used to sing carols in the patients' common room, and many of the patients used to join in the singing. We've often wondered since, why some of the people there were patients. Quite a few of them were allowed out unattended. They were very well known and liked throughout the village. Before the run–down, the gardens and grounds were kept immaculate, and the hospital was virtually self–sufficient regards vegetables'.

Children were sent to buy 'lunatic dripping' at 5½d a pound, from Mrs Maggs, the cook.

'The majority of the patients were either wealthy or had wealthy relatives and most were middle aged or elderly'.

'I knew some of the people who were patients at the House. One lady came to many of our whist drives. We often saw patients out with their nurses, or attendants, but some seemed worse than others, but always polite when we met them, but of course, we all knew that there were some very bad cases.'

'The village then, [in 1940s] was very small to what it has become now. There were quite a few Irish families where the parents worked at Laverstock House'.

The late Ernest Norton, who came to the village when he was seven

Entrance to Laverstock House on left, just beyond cottage; looking up The Avenue c1910 (photograph private collection)

The White House (the medical superintendent's house) now demolished, on Riverside Road, photograph 1890s, WSA 3433/1/38

in 1910 recalled, 'Half way up Duck Lane, there was a pump station which used to make the electricity and pump the water for Laverstock Park ... The patients used to go to St Andrew's Church ... And then there was a Rev – and he was a resident up there and he often used to read the lesson. He used to come to our house and take our dog out for walks. They were

The White Cottage (the doctor's house), now 'Kerrycroy', on Riverside Road, photograph 1890s, WSA3433/1/38

all private patients ... Some of the patients were very bad. Most of the nurses were Irish. The kitchen staff were all locals ... The House was a nice looking place. There was a pagoda in the gardens where the patients could go to sit and relax. That's when they were alright of course but the majority of the time you could hear them bawling and shouting'... Dr Benson (medical superintendent 1925–1938) lived in the 'White House', which is now pulled down ... next to the 'White Cottage'. Miss Haynes and Paul Haynes lived in a big thatched cottage ('The Avenue'). The whole of the island belonged to the asylum.'

'Dr Horace Hill (1939–1953), the medical superintendent), later lived in 'The White House' and another doctor, (Dr Neil Mackinnon, physician and surgeon), lived in 'The White Cottage'.

'I must say that the grounds and out houses at Laverstock Park were kept beautifully. After Dr Hill died in 1953, the ownership passed to his wife... In 1955 the whole lot, House, grounds and all were put up for sale. We were quite distressed at the time'. [43]

The late Dr John Norris was the last visiting doctor from about 1948–55, calling every day and writing certificates for the patients. The institution went bankrupt in 1955, the hospital was demolished and 42 houses were built in the grounds. Dr Norris confirmed that the staff was mainly Irish RC nurses who lived in Laverstock, but the head male nurse was a Scot, while the matron was an Irish Protestant! In the 1950s padded cells still existed, then called 'seclusion' and there were fenced areas where patients could go outside but not be able to escape. At its closure in 1955 all the patients were dispersed, some to the Old Manor which had been taken over by the NHS in 1954. [44]

principal, but considered it 'ignominious' that she should be so confined. [41]

By 1901, still under Dr Manning, there were just 48 patients, normally with 'no occupation' and 15 servants including five mental nurses, all female and young. Details of admissions for 1904 include full medical details and reports of the patients, some violent or suicidal. A printed, signed declaration from the visitors stated that they should 'keep secret all such matters as should come to knowledge in the execution of my office'. [42] There are no available records after 1913 because of the 100 year closure on medical records under the Data Protection Act. In the 1920s and 1930s, as in other private mental homes, some patients were almost certainly suffering from the traumas of the First World War, especially shell shock.

Despite the obvious propaganda, and there were contradictory reports, there is much to be proud of Laverstock's mental health record. The Finch family, moving from non–medical to medically qualified proprietors, believed in preventative treatment in a quiet, rural environment away from the stresses of city life. The emphasis on minimal restraint and rehabilitation ensured that Laverstock was among the most progressive of the early 19th century asylums while the careful selection of attendants and their supervision proved an important precedent to the modern profession of mental nursing.

Ruth Newman is the co–author with Jane Howells, of Salisbury Past *and in 2011 they edited and transcribed 'William Small's, Cherished Memories and Associations', volume 64 of the Wiltshire Record Society. She lives in a house on the site of the former asylum.*

Bibliography & Abbreviations

SJ = Salisbury and Winchester Journal
VCH = Victoria County History
Anon, 1860, *Our holiday at Laverstock Park Asylum; how we visited Stonehenge and what we learned there.* London: John Churchill
Beattie, William, 1855, *Life and letters of Thomas Campbell, Vol 2,* Harper & Brothers. Reprinted 2012 Forgotten Books
Mackenzie, Charlotte, 1992, *Psychiatry for the Rich: A History of Ticehurst Private Asylum 1792–1917.* Wellcome Institute Series in the History of Medicine, Routledge
Parry–Jones, William, 1972, *The trade in lunacy: a study of private madhouses in England in the eighteenth and nineteenth centuries:* Routledge and Kegan Paul
Parrett, Sylvia, 1999, *Laverstock, from Victoria to the Fifties,* Parrett
Smith, Gertrude, 1982, *The Old Manor Hospital, Salisbury, Wiltshire: private madhouse, licensed house, psychiatric hospital,* Smith

At the Wiltshire and Swindon Archives [WSA]
A1/560/9 Admission Registers, Laverstock House, 1797–1955, with minutes 1828–45
A1/561 Annual Reports of Licensed Houses, 1829–31
A1/562/6 Plans of Licensed Houses, Laverstock House, 1829–1844
A1/563 Certificates of admission etc 1834–35
A1/564 Miscellaneous including Laverstock House Pauper Dietary 1847
499/27 Britford: St Peter, Overseers of the Poor, volume with various documents, 1715–1822,
1020/108 Longbridge Deverell St Peter and St Paul with Crockerton Holy Trinity, Receipted bill for the cost of maintenance of Benjamin Whillard (or Wheeler) a lunatic, at Mr William Finch's house in Laverstock, 1813–14
1861/1 Laverstock House prospectus, 1824?

Notes

1 Smith, prologue and Parrett, 15 both have 'after 1754' for its founding; VCH V, 329 suggests the 1760s

2   *SJ*, 3 December 1770; p1, *SJ*, 1 July 1771, p3; South, Mary, Southampton, Salisbury and Winchester's smallpox inoculation campaigns; *The Local Historian*, Vol 43, No2, May 2013. Salisbury was an early centre for the prevention of smallpox through inoculation, a deliberate exposure to a mild form of the virus in order to create a localised infection and thus generate immunity against further infection. The (Daniel) Sutton method was safer and involved a shallow scratch and careful selection of mildly affected donors.

3   *SJ*, 31 March 1777, p3

4   *SJ*, 8 February 1779, p2

5   *SJ*, 9 August 1784, p2

6   *SJ*, 31 December 1798, p4

7   *SJ*, 7 January 1799, p4

8   *SJ*, 01 October 1810, p4

9   WSA A1/560/9 *Register or List of the several insane persons confined in the House of Mr William Finch and Mr James Lacy at Laverstock … licensed for the reception of lunatics*

10 WSA A1/563 medical certificates 1834–5

11 *The Pheasant Inn* lioness, www.iolfree.ie/~dorsetbigcats/marcushistory.htm, accessed 2013; Campbell, 145–6

12 *The Times*, 26 May 1838, p6

13 Thomas Campbell, (1777–1844), poet, Carnall, Geoffrey, ODNB

14 Campbell, 139–140

15 *Ibid*, 141

16 Probably John Hillier, 'well–known' cook to Dr Finch at asylum from 1815–1848. Described as a 'man of colour', he died just two weeks after Finch, *SJ*, 22 January 1848, p4

17 Campbell, 140–146; extracts from a letter written on 15/16 October 1822, from Campbell to a friend

18 *Ibid*, 147, 154, 162–3. By 1828, after Campbell's wife's death, his son appears to be living briefly with him in Richmond, but in a letter of 29 June 1828 he describes placing Thomas in Dr Allen's progressive High Beach private asylum where the poet John Clare was a patient. Thomas remained there until the summer of 1844, shortly after his father had been buried in 'Poets Corner' in Westminster Abbey. He appeared before the Commission of Lunacy and so impressed the jury that he was declared 'of sound mind'. He lived independently, on private means (probably the allowance left for his care by his father), for nearly 40 years, with no evidence of insanity, dying in 1882.

19 WSA 1861/1; Minutes of evidence 1815 Select Commission, p22, quoted in Parry–Jones, 198

20 *SJ*, 12 September 1814, p1

21 Letter from W Finch MD, 25 November 1837, *The London Medical Gazette* 1837–8, Vol 21, 333

22 WSA A1/561; the visitors were Wadham Wyndham MP, Edward Duke and eminent Salisbury surgeon, Richard Fowler

23 WSA A1/560/9

24 *Ibid*

25 WSA A1/562/6; the general layout of the grounds remained essentially unchanged until 1950 except for the addition of another doctor's house, a large thatched cottage, 'The Avenue', the home of the Haynes family.

26 WSA 1861/1

27 WSA A1/561, 1829 Report: General Observations by Visitors on Condition of Patients and State of the Establishment. Little is known of James Lacy 'gentleman', the co–proprietor of Laverstock House, a wealthy non–medical partner. In 1824 the three directors were Dr Finch, Mr James Lacy, junior and Henry Coates, well known Salisbury surgeon at the infirmary. Coates retired in 1827 and Lacy died in 1839
www.london–gazette.co.uk/issues/18379/pages/1542/page.pdf and
www.london-gazette.co.uk/issues/19855/pages/1184/page.pdf, accessed 2013
28 WSA 499/27
29 WSA 499/27
30 WSA 1020/108
31 *SJ*, 12 September 1814, p1
32 Campbell, 144
33 WSA A1/563
34 WSA A1/564
35 *SJ*, 9 July 1832, p3
36 1881 England census on Ancestry.co.uk. In 1841 Laverstock and Fisherton asylums had been of comparable size but the latter kept its pauper intake and became, by 1881, the largest private House ever known, with 672 patients including 542 pauper and criminal lunatics. In the censuses (1841–1901), age, sex and former occupations (where known) were recorded but just initials to preserve patients' (and families') privacy. Only in 1861 were names and full details of place of birth given as well.
37 *SJ*, 22 January 1848, p4. Dr William Corbin Finch (1804–1867), the son of Charles, continued the family link at Fisherton Asylum where he was proprietor and also senior physician at Salisbury Infirmary.
38 *SJ*, 21 July 1855, p2
39 Anon, 1860. *Our holiday at Laverstock Park Asylum;* article 'Medical Merrymaking', *Hampshire Advertiser,* 11 Aug, 1860, p4
40 *books.google.com.ar/books/about/Reports_from_Commissioners.htm...* accessed 2013; VCH 5, 329; Report of Commissioners in Lunacy, 1862, 45–6; Parrett, 20–21
41 Hoare, P, 2005, *England's Lost Eden. Adventures in Victorian Utopia;* and widely reported; WSA A1/560/9
42 WSA A1/563 certificates of admission
43 Much of this information from former village residents comes from interviews in 1985 undertaken by Gill Newman as part of a university project on Laverstock Asylum
44 Information kindly supplied by Dr John Norris to the author in June 2008

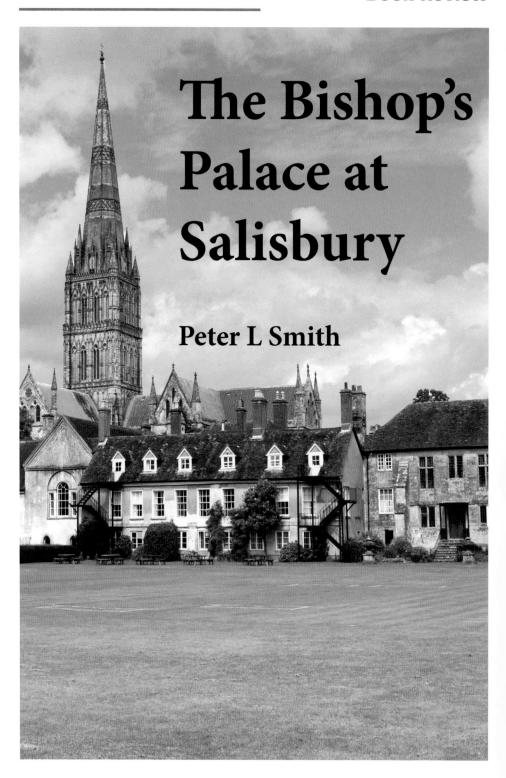

The Bishop's
Palace at
Salisbury

Peter L Smith

Book Review

The Bishop's Palace at Salisbury by Peter L Smith,
(Spire Books Ltd, Reading), 2013
224pp hardback, 21 colour and 96 b/w illustrations,
160mm x 240mm. £29.95
ISBN 9781904965411

Well written and beautifully illustrated, with numerous colour photographs, this attractive book by Peter L Smith, the former History Co–ordinator and Librarian of Salisbury Cathedral School, provides a concise study of the Bishop's Palace, a building which has played a significant role in Salisbury's past. The author's extensive research into the Palace and School archives for over 30 years has unearthed a rich treasury of stories and information to delight both the general reader and to provide an invaluable resource for the local historian.

Salisbury's Bishop's Palace was the home of the Bishops of Salisbury for eight centuries and an integral part of the creation of the new city of Salisbury from the early 13th century. The book provides a concise chronology of how the building has evolved from 1225 when the first phase was completed. The various alterations made to the architecture and interior structures are also described along with the changing uses of the building made to meet the needs of the Episcopal residents and, since 1947, the pupils of Salisbury Cathedral School.

During early medieval times the Bishops of Salisbury led peripatetic lives, visiting their different residences in Wiltshire, Dorset and London. The book highlights how the Palace at Salisbury served primarily as accommodation for the bishop and his officials when visiting Salisbury and for entertaining important guests, attending King Richard II's Parliament, held here in 1384. Later architectural changes made in the 15th century by Bishop Beauchamp resulted in a more comfortable family residence being created, which was of vital importance following the Reformation.

The Palace required major reconstruction after the Civil War when Bishop Beauchamp's Great Hall was demolished. Bishop Seth Ward sought advice from

Sir Christopher Wren regarding the rebuilding of the Great Hall, the East Tower and the southern range. A significant incident in British history occurred at the Bishop's Palace in November 1685. William of Orange and his troops had landed at Torbay and were making progress eastwards when King James II arrived at Salisbury. The King suffered a debilitating nosebleed which lasted three days. During this time his trusted commanders deserted him and the King retreated to London and into exile abroad. The new monarchs, King William and Mary were joyously received into the City of London a few days later.

The book highlights the lives of prominent Bishops of Salisbury who lived in the Palace during the 18th and 19th centuries and influenced the appearance of the building today. Bishop Shute Barrington was responsible for the restoration of the grand rooms which were used for entertaining Royal guests such as the visits of King George III during his journeys to Weymouth. Bishop John Fisher, the friend and patron of John Constable entertained the artist here in 1811 and 1816, commissioning the painting of 'Salisbury Cathedral from the Bishop's Grounds', which illustrates the landscaping features that he had created.

During the bishoprics of George Moberly and John Wordsworth, the Palace became the home of two upper–class Victorian families. The book includes glimpses of their lives as recorded by Charlotte Anne Moberly and Elizabeth Wordsworth. After 1911, the bishops who resided here faced a growing financial problem in maintaining the building without a large domestic staff. From 1947, the building was adapted to become the present home of Salisbury Cathedral School.

This most readable and excellently produced book is the first comprehensive study of the Bishop's Palace and an important addition to Salisbury's local history archive. Highly recommended.

Margaret Smith

The Salisbury Community Choir's Big Birthday

John Elliott

Around 1990 the Women's Rock Music Co-operative started organising singing workshops in Salisbury under the banner *Free the Voice*. By 1992 this had led to a class run by Salisbury College called *Singing for Non–Singers* which in turn led to a group forming a choir called *Untrained Voices*. From all of this emerged what is now the Salisbury Community Choir which celebrates its 21st birthday this year.

For the first few years the Salisbury Community Choir was about 40 strong and was led by Jan Hughes. Then late in 1998 Jan resigned and Fiona Clarke was appointed as Musical Director with Ann Dean as Chairman, Margaret Fleming as Secretary and Ron Collins as Treasurer. Twenty years later Ann still sings with the choir and Fiona runs the Salisbury based Babes & Ballads. In many ways this was a crucial moment for the SCC. Fiona brought a new energy to the rehearsals

First known photograph of the choir. Ann Dean Collection. Origin unknown.

The SCC at Chafyn Grove School (Ash Mills).

and concerts, along with a dose of her unique sense of humour. Things moved up a notch musically and the choir became more competent and more ambitious.

Regular concerts were held in local churches, at Stourhead Gardens, a lunchtime concert in St Paul's Cathedral and even a concert in the cattle ring at the livestock market! In 2001 the choir launched its first overseas tour with a visit to Germany, and tours to Paris and Poland followed, along with a surge in membership. In 2004 the choir took on its biggest challenge yet, when it decided to perform Karl Jenkins' *The Armed Man: A Mass for Peace* in Salisbury Cathedral. This was a huge undertaking as previously the longest piece of music the choir had tackled was the 'Hallelujah Chorus' from Handel's *Messiah*.

After months of intense work the concert was an amazing success. There was a full house and an opening speech by Rev Colin Jones, the then Dean of Cape Town Cathedral, whom Desmond Tutu had asked to represent him. Taking the title of the Karl Jenkins piece as his key Colin Jones reflected on how most of the major nations spent vast sums on military academies but nothing on an academy devoted to the search for peace. Before departing he suggested that the choir should travel to Cape Town and perform the work there as part of Desmond Tutu's efforts to raise the funds to build a Peace Centre in Cape Town and to celebrate the end of apartheid and the formation of the new South Africa.

Much planning followed and in 2007 about 110 members of the choir set out on what was to be a great adventure. There were concerts in Cape Town's St George's Cathedral, at the Waterfront, at Elsie's River (a coloured township) and in Gugulethu (a large black township near the airport), plus a massive concert in Cape Town's City Hall where the SCC, together with three local choirs, performed the African premiere of *The Armed Man*. Later a smaller group drawn from these choirs performed the same work in Carnegie Hall, New York.

It was always hoped that during the trip the choir would get to see parts of South Africa that tourists normally never visit. A preliminary contact had been made with the Fezeka High School in Gugulethu, and despite some reservations, one morning the whole party set out in coaches for the township. So started a day that was to have profound implications for the future of the choir.

Gugulethu was formed to take the overflow black population after the blacks and coloureds had been forcibly ejected from the centre of Cape Town as part of the apartheid land clearances. The best houses are about the size of a British double garage, the worst are made of scraps of timber, metal and polythene. In the midst of this the Fezeka High School attempts to provide a secondary education and an English teacher, Phume Tsewu, ran an after school choir. The young people showed the choir members around the school and the township

Fezeka School choir with Desmond Tutu in Salisbury.

Fezeka performing in the Close as part of the Salisbury International Arts Festival 2008.

and then everyone gathered at a church for an evening joint concert. They sang, we sang and we sang together. The audience cheered, clapped and shouted and we all became struck by the wonderful voices of the black students, only to hear that there was no prospect of them ever developing their voices because they could never afford to go to the University of Cape Town Opera School.

That evening the Fezeka Scholarship Fund was born. This is now an independent Salisbury based charity that raises money to help fund the costs associated with disadvantaged South African students studying at university or on vocational courses. So far the charity has raised over £120,000 and supported about 25 students.

The combined efforts of the Salisbury Festival, the Donald Gordon Foundation, Wales Millennium Centre, a private donor and the SCC resulted in a 77 strong party from the Fezeka High School visiting Salisbury in 2008. They stayed with SCC members and together performed in Salisbury Cathedral and in the Wales Millennium Centre.

At the end of 2009 Fiona decided that she had taken the choir as far as she could and resigned as Musical Director. Her replacement is Jeremy Backhouse, a choral director of national standing who had just moved to Salisbury. Jeremy is Musical Director of Vivace which was formed from the Guildford Philharmonic Choir and who perform regularly in Guildford Cathedral and on a less regular basis in the Royal Albert Hall. He also runs Vasari who are one of the top UK chamber choirs and have an international reputation.

Under Jeremy the SCC played a major part in the Salisbury Chilcott Project which commissioned Bob Chilcott to write and then perform the Salisbury Vespers in Salisbury Cathedral. Two performances within the Salisbury Festival and two European tours have followed along with a CD, but the highpoint of 2013 will be the concert in Salisbury Cathedral on 12 October.

For this the SCC will be joined by the SAYM [Salisbury Area Young Musicians] children's choir, some of South Wilts Grammar School's A Capella Choir and three choristers from the Cathedral choir. The first half of the concert will be the world premiere of *The City Garden*, a new work commissioned by the SCC. It is composed by Will Todd, who was also responsible for *The Call of Wisdom* that featured in the Diamond Jubilee Thanksgiving Service and was recorded by Tenebrae with the English Chamber Orchestra. Will's music encompasses a wide range of musical styles and genres – from jazz to contemporary liturgical music.

The City Garden is a magical story of ecological renewal and awakening and takes us on a romantic journey through the seasons; different moods, temperatures and weather supply the dramatic light and shade of this work. Our spiritual life is like a city garden. It endures its seasons, is blessed by nature's magical renewal, and it evolves its own boundaries with the demands of modernity. It is arranged in four movements, one for each season and starts with Autumn.

The second half of the concert will be a performance of Benjamin Britten's *Saint Nicolas*. Written in 1948 for the centennial celebrations of Lancing College, Sussex, it marks his first professional work intended primarily for performance by amateur musicians. Britten scored the piece for mixed choir, tenor soloist, three or four boys, strings, piano duet, organ and percussion. It is now frequently performed by youth and amateur ensembles. Eric Crozier wrote the lyrics after extensive research into the legendary life of Saint Nicholas, who was Bishop of Myra, Lycia. In the performance the choir represent the contemporary people, and they call to Nicolas to speak to them across the ages. As the piece progresses so does the dialogue, with interjections by angels and others.

The concert will be a fitting way to mark the choir's 21st anniversary – a celebration of community music and a demonstration of what can be achieved with hard work and determination.

All photographs are by the author unless otherwise specified.

The 8th Lord Arundell by George Romney. The National Portrait Gallery.

Relics, Rumours and Research

Barry Williamson

On Monday 21 November 2011 *The Guardian* contained a full page article by Charlotte Higgins about a forthcoming exhibition at The Ashmolean Museum in Oxford. It was to consist of nearly 150 exhibits from the cargo of the *Westmorland*, a British ship captured on 7 January 1779 by two French warships near Malaga. The ship was on its way from Livorno in Italy to London and besides the normal cargo of anchovies, olives, biscuits and Parmesan cheese, contained 68 crates full of the paintings, sculpture, books, prints and luxury shopping acquired by British aristocrats and gentlemen on the Grand Tour. The context of the attack was the outbreak of war between Britain and France in February 1778 as a result of France making an alliance with the rebellious American colonists. The title of the exhibition was to be: *The English Prize: the Capture of the* Westmorland, *An Episode of the Grand Tour.*

The penultimate paragraph stated: 'on board was a collection of saint's relics, concealed (bound as they were for Protestant England) within a marble plinth. They had been hidden there by an English Jesuit based in Rome, John Thorpe, who was sending them to the Earl of Arundel, a prominent English Catholic. After the *Westmorland*'s capture, a Papal nuncio had to scramble to get them back before they were unknowingly sold.'

However the Earl of Arundel (heir to the Duke of Norfolk and not connected with the Arundells of Wardour) was a lukewarm Catholic and actually joined the Church of England in 1780 at the time of the Gordon Riots. It was hardly probable that he would be collecting relics! The nobleman in question was far more likely to be the 8th Lord Arundell, whose agent in Rome, Father Thorpe, (from 1768 to his death in 1791) played a crucial role in acquiring the pictures and works of art to fill the new mansion at Wardour. A superb collection of over 200 letters from him to Lord Arundell exists among the family archives. Although the correspondence is one-sided and none of Arundell's letters has survived it is

Aerial view of Wardour Castle taken in 1934. The chapel is in the west wing on the right of the picture. By courtesy of Major General Patrick Fagan CB, MBE.

a rich source, full of material about buying works of art and Catholic affairs in Rome.

This was a red herring too exciting to resist. I therefore wrote to *The Guardian* and the Curator of the exhibition at the Ashmolean, Dr Catherine Whistler, asking whether a mistake had been made. They confirmed that it had and that the writer had mixed up Arundel and Arundell. A check of Thorpe's letters in the Arundell archives at the History Centre in Chippenham[1] for references to the relics revealed a complicated story of the despatch of the relics, their disappearance, negotiation, rumour and eventual triumph when the marble plinth containing the relics reached Wardour in April 1789, ten years late. This information was passed on to Dr Whistler who replied that the Spanish Director of the research project, Professor Jose Maria Luzon Nogué, would be delighted to hear the news but dismayed because he had just completed the chapter on the loss of the relics for the magnificent catalogue that was to accompany the exhibition in Oxford and the USA.[2] It was about to be printed. Its final (now inaccurate) paragraph read:

> 'The relics that Father Thorpe had hoped to provide for the inaugural Mass in the chapel at Wardour Castle – which was held by Bishop Charles Walmesley, Vicar Apostolic of the Western District in November 1776 – were still in

Madrid twelve years later and their present location is unknown. The *Corpo Santo* (the Holy Body, as Thorpe always called the relics) that Pope Clement XIII sent as a gift to Lord Arundell never reached Wardour Castle.'

Thorpe's letters told a different story but was it too late to make alterations? Would the information be seen as unwelcome interference from an outsider? Not at all. From the beginning, Dr Whistler and Professor Luzon welcomed my research and included me as a late arrival to the *Westmorland* family. The printing was halted. A further visit was made to Chippenham to collect the year-by-year references in the letters to the extraordinary story of the survival and rescue of the relics and the data sent to Professor Luzon who rewrote the chapter.

It is worth noting at this point how the project began. In 1999 Professor Luzon assembled a team in Madrid to explore the history of the museum collections in Spain. It was known that many objects had arrived in the 18th century from a captured ship but there were no details. The inventory of this ship was found in the Academy archives[3] in Madrid. Many items had initials beside them such as H.R.H.D.G., F.B., G.M., T.HD., E.D.. What did they mean and where had

Chapel of the new castle, consecrated in November 1776. Photograph by the author, by courtesy of Lord Talbot of Malahide.

the ship come from? The Spanish bureaucrats kept meticulous records and their inventory listed 778 items that arrived in the Academy Museum in Madrid in 1784 and from there were dispersed to the royal palaces and to 12 Spanish museums. The whole collection was valued at the enormous sum of £100,000 (about £7 million in today's values). A caretaker, Juan Morenco had written a description of each item as it arrived. The books and prints sent to the academy had PY written on them. Another mystery.

The most valuable item in the whole consignment was 'The Liberation of Andromeda by Perseus' painted by Anton Raphael Mengs. The picture had passed fairly rapidly to the collection of Catherine the Great of Russia and was in the Hermitage. The caretaker's long list included 'Item No 7: A crate that contains A Marble Pedestal that according to what is said contains the Body of a Martyr Saint and has not been opened.' This was where the breakthrough came. Another document in the same bundle was found in the Academy archives. It was a memo from Father Thorpe to the Spanish ambassador at the Vatican, the Marques de Nibbiano, written in early 1784. It was a record of a meeting they had held in Rome at which Thorpe petitioned for the protection of these relics and Nibbiano promised to use 'his interest' to help recover them. Thorpe's memo told the whole story; the name of the ship, its capture, the storage of the 778 objects in Malaga and their transfer to Madrid:

> 'Memorandum to the marques de Nibbiano. A small box in crimson silk containing relics of a holy martyr, a personal gift from His Holiness Clement XIII to His Excellency My lord Arundell of Great Britain in order to be sent to London (where such things if discovered by the Customs would be burned), was skilfully inserted inside a large piece of marble, called yellow Siena marble … and the whole placed in a wooden crate marked T.HD. No 7; Florence MacCarty and Son at Livorno had this crate loaded onto the ship the *Westmorland* with the English Captain Willis Mackell in the year 1778, which ship as it had left the port was taken captive in the Mediterranean and brought to Malaga. Then Signor Duca Grimaldi, as requested by the Prince Rezzonico, Roman senator asked the Governor of Malaga so that in the sale of the crate, preference would be given to the agent of Lord Arundell. But by command of His Most Catholic Majesty, all of the Marbles, Paintings and similar items were without exception, at the King's expense, transported from Malaga to Madrid, thus the writer Father Thorpe turns to Your Excellency, supplicating him to use his valuable office at the Court so that the said crate should be released on request and implores that the marble container should not be opened and the small box should not be removed.'

Nibbiano had passed the memo to the Spanish Prime Minister, Conde do Floridablanca who had passed it to the Academy where it was acted on. The objects not wanted by the King were transferred to the Academy for use in

Reynold's portrait of James Paine and his son in 1764, five years before he began work on the new mansion at Wardour. The Ashmolean Museum, Oxford University.

teaching. It was discovered that the letters PY stood for Presa Ynglesa or the English Prize, the term by which the collection was known. Crate No 7 was never opened. Professor Luzon's team then began research into the owners of the crates, the Grand Tourists who had been on this most expensive of shopping expeditions and were sending home purchases to fill their mansions – His Royal Highness the Duke of Gloucester (H.R.H.D.G., brother of King George III), George Legge, Viscount Lewisham (addressed to his father, the Earl of Dartmouth, E.D.), Sir John Henderson of Fordell (F.D.), Frances Basset (F.B.), heir to a Cornish tin mine fortune and many others. T.HD. stood for Thomas Hornyold, a Catholic banker who acted as agent for Lord Arundell in London. Nothing more could be discovered about Crate No 7 despite research into copies of some of Thorpe's letters in the Brinsley Ford collection at the Paul Mellon Centre in London.[4] Hence the conclusion that the relics never reached Wardour. For some reason the research team was completely unaware of the Thorpe letters in the Arundell archives at Chippenham.

Henry the 8th Lord Arundell was one of the richest men in 18th century England. He had estates in seven counties with a small London estate and an annual income of about £4.5 million, in today's values. His great project was the

The 8th Lord Arundell on the Grand Tour in 1760. Christie's Images Ltd.

building of a new mansion at Wardour between 1769 and 1776, to the designs of James Paine. It was the largest Georgian mansion in Wiltshire. It is regarded as Paine's masterpiece and especially the magnificent chapel in the west wing, the most splendid Catholic chapel to be built in England since the Reformation.

Father John Thorpe was a Jesuit priest from Yorkshire where he owned land near Halifax. He had been Henry's teacher at St Omers, the college in northeast France where rich English Catholic families sent their children to be educated. He moved to Rome in 1756 and spent time with Henry on his Grand Tour visit in 1760. He was a reluctant art agent but had plenty of spare time after the Pope disbanded the Jesuit Order in 1773. For example, between 1771 and 1774 he sent 196 pictures to Wardour, mostly copies of works by the great masters and all 'with a strict regard for decency and their nudities decently covered' as he noted with some amusement.[5] He was particularly involved with the furnishing of the chapel ready for its consecration in 1776.

Pope Clement XIII was one of the most attractive of 18th century Popes – kind, generous, accessible and humble. He came from a noble Venetian family, the Rezzonicos and was so surprised to be elected Pope in 1758 that he took to his bed for a week. His mother died of a heart attack on hearing the news. Henry

Arundell must have met him while he lived in Rome on his Grand Tour and established a close rapport with him. The pope promised Henry important relics for the altar of his new chapel. (Relics were believed to be essential for a Catholic altar because they imparted a divine blessing on the building.) The Pope died in 1769 and Thorpe sent Henry a lock of his hair, removed on his deathbed.

What story does the Thorpe correspondence at Chippenham tell? Ten letters refer to the relics and their journey. The first reference is in a letter dated 30 November 1776. Thorpe is sending the *Corpo Santo* to Lord Arundell on a ship called *Hannanel* under Captain James Meads, 'in a box of common wood covered with two cases of oil cloth … no clue that it belongs to your Lordship.'[6] Then silence until 3 July 1778 when a Bill of Lading is sent to Wardour stating that the case marked T. HD. No 7 had been shipped by Florence MacCarty and Son 'in and upon the good Ship called *Westmorland* whereof is Master under God for this present voyage, Willis Mackell and now riding at anchor in this Port of Leghorn and by God's grace bound for London.' At the bottom is written 'One case cont. a Marble pedestal well conditioned for acct as p. Factory. Content unknown, Willis Mackell.'[7] But why the change from the *Hannanel* to the *Westmorland* and the two years delay? Perhaps Capt Meads refused to carry the cargo on learning what it really contained. Taking relics to England was too risky in the volatile anti-Catholic atmosphere of London in the 1770s.

On 25 July 1778, Thorpe was able to send Arundell an optimistic report: 'The

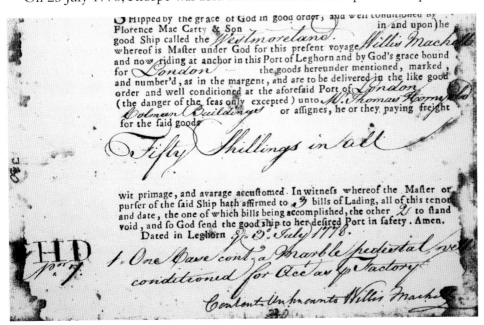

Bill of Lading issued for Case No 7 on the *Westmorland*. Photograph by the author, by courtesy of the Wiltshire and Swindon History Centre.

Cpo Sto [*Corpo Santo*] is now out on the sea [not true, the ship did not leave until December 1778]. The block of marble is large because a lesser piece would have been made too thin by the excavation necessary for inserting the box of Relicks …The cavity is also so artfully closed up by a strong panel of the same marble as to be not discoverable. The marble is *Giabladi di Sienna Brecciato*, three sides of it are squared and polished, it is in the form of a great pedestal … the bottom of it is rough and faced with sea sand and there the opening must be found … it may safely be cut up for panels of chimney pieces, tables or the like.'[8]

Then all is confusion as Thorpe waited in Rome to hear of the cargo's safe arrival. On 28 June 1780 he wrote to Arundell that he had had a report from Malaga; the cargo was there and McCarty the agent was trying to locate and secure Case No 7. Eighteen months later, Thorpe reported that the case had been discovered and he would ask Prince Rezzonico[9] to use his influence to rescue it. Nothing more until October 1783 when Thorpe passed on the bad news that King Carlos III had paid for the whole cargo, including Case No 7, to be removed at his expense to Madrid as a prize of war. Spain had declared war on Britain in June 1779. Prince Rezzonico was contacted again. Soon after this in early 1784 Thorpe wrote the memo to the Spanish ambassador which proved so crucial in unravelling the story.

On 16 April 1788 Thorpe wrote in a gloomy mood. He lamented the 'past, fruitless transactions', admitted the whereabouts of the marble was a mystery but announced a new rescue plan if it could be found. It was to be sent in the diplomatic bag to the Spanish ambassador in London, 'although it is probably irrecoverable in any condition to enjoy it.'[10] But only a month later there was better news. The *Corpo Santo* had been found in Madrid; Prince Rezzonico planned to ask the Papal Nuncio to take delivery of it and send it to the Venetian Resident in London. 'Thus I hope for a happy issue of the business which I have always numbered among the many unlucky accidents in the last war.'[11]

Finally, a triumphant letter on 22 April 1789. Lord Arundell had obviously told Thorpe of the delivery at Wardour of Case No 7. ' … the safe arrival of the *Cpo Sto* at Wardour after so many years of bondage in Spain is also a subject of some congratulation to me. For bringing it out of the Case please to observe that side of the Marble which is rough and perhaps yet has sand sticking to it; if this side be well scraped with a chisel or like instrument, the seams of the square cavity will appear and the thin marble slab that closes that cavity being broken or lifted up, will discover the Tin Box wherein lies the *Cpo Sto* covered with crimson silk and bound with ribands and seals is lodged. This Tin Box, by inverting the block of marble may be turned out of the cavity and then be unsoldered to come to the Relicks. If they be afterwards placed in the Urn under the Altar on the back part of the Urn, the following inscription, if your Lordship approves it, may be put in letters of gilt bronze in one or more lines:

> CORPUS S. CLEMENTIS M. CLEMENTIS XIII P. M. DONUM [the body
> of St Clement the Martyr, the gift of Pope Clement XIII][12]

Why was so much secrecy necessary to conceal the import of relics to England? It is important to remember that this was the time of the Penal Laws which lasted from 1559 until Catholic Emancipation in 1829. They were designed to make the practice of the Catholic faith very difficult without risking fines and imprisonment. It has been an English habit to shrug off the laws as if they were only on the statute book and not operational but that is not true. For more than 250 years, England's green and pleasant land was a land of persecution for the Catholic minority on account of their religion. As a Catholic, Henry Arundell was prevented by Acts of Parliament from attending a Catholic school in England; from attending an English university, from holding any public office, locally or nationally; from serving in the Army or Navy or in law or medicine; and from being baptised, married or buried in any other than an Anglican church. Officially he was not allowed to hear Mass freely or to employ a Catholic priest for the very large Catholic community at Wardour[13] or to provide a place of Catholic worship for them but there were Jesuit priests at Wardour from at least 1598 onwards.

With regard to relics, a 1606 law forbade the import of 'crucifixes, emblems and relics relating to the Popish religion.' Thorpe was taking a risk in sending the cargo to England. But the particularly volatile atmosphere of the 1770s made matters much worse. Catholics had always been seen in popular imagination as representing autocracy and as a threat to English Liberty. Brave Protestant England had fought through the centuries for survival against continental Catholic countries and won. The Jacobites represented the greatest threat in the 18th century. If they should win, English Liberty was lost. But things were changing. The defeat of Bonnie Prince Charlie in 1746 at Culloden made that unlikely. When the Old Pretender died in January 1766, Pope Clement XIII (Henry's friend) refused to recognise the inebriated Bonnie Prince Charlie as King Charles III. He recognised the Hanoverians as lawful Kings of England.

Over the next few years a remarkable rapprochement took place. The Pope received personally any relative of George III visiting Rome. Father Booth, rector of the English College in Rome, was expelled from Rome by the Pope in April 1766 for referring to Prince Charles as King of England and to his chair as a throne when he said Mass with the Prince present. Thorpe complained in a letter to Henry, 'there is no regard here for Catholicks, the Protestants are the first in favour and to whom nothing is to be refused.'[14] There were rumours that King George III had converted to the Catholic faith. He was nicknamed Pope George in the streets of London. It might be expected that public opinion

A cartoon of King George III attending mass. The British Museum.

in Britain would greet the dawn of religious toleration with overwhelming joy. Not at all. Reactionary elements saw this as a threat to Liberty. Then two parliamentary acts made matters worse. In 1774 the Quebec Act gave Catholics in the newly conquered province of Quebec, official toleration for their religious beliefs. In 1778 a Catholic Relief Act was passed granting Catholics a new Oath of Allegiance containing words more acceptable to their beliefs and freedom for Catholic priests and teachers. The motive was not a sudden government conversion to liberal values but a desperate need to gain more recruits for the army to fight the American rebels.

The atmosphere in London became volatile. English Liberty was at stake. The war against the American rebels and their French and Spanish allies was going badly. The French fleet dominated the Channel. There were rumours of an imminent invasion. Anti-royal posters appeared in the London streets:

'Proceed, great Sir! And, breaking all restraint,
Embrace the scarlet whore, and be a Saint.
Sworn to maintain the establishe'd Church, advance
The cross of Rome, the miracles of France.'[15]

A cartoon handed out in London showed the king attending Mass. Luther's picture is torn, the Pope's picture takes pride of place. Protestant petitions lie on the floor of the King's privy. His wicked ministers Lords North and Sandwich have their portraits in places of honour.[16] Then came the anti-Catholic Gordon Riots in June 1780. They were the worst outbreak of civil disorder in modern Britain. Dozens of rioters died in London.

All this was the atmosphere in which Thorpe attempted to send the relics to Wardour. News of events in London must have reached him in Rome and explains why an ordinary wooden box had to be abandoned and a marble pedestal with a secret cavity substituted. Relics were a cargo loaded with risk and provocation.

Back to the exhibition: Dr Whistler, as a good historian, insisted that a letter written in 1789 was no proof that the relics had actually remained at Wardour. Were they still in the chapel? A letter to Lord Talbot of Malahide, chairman of the trustees of the chapel and owner of the Wardour estate, asking if he knew about the relics, received a negative reply and an invitation to meet him after Mass on 17 January 2012 to search for them. The priest, the sacristan and a friend from Bristol were also present. The search began behind and under the altar. No urn, no cupboard where they might be kept. But against the right wall behind the altar was a small gilt cabinet with a glass front, covered with a velvet curtain. Lord Talbot sent the sacristan to collect a bunch of keys from the vestry. None fitted. A cheque card failed too. Then another bunch of keys provided one that fitted. The cabinet contained 18 small locket cases each showing a fragment of bone or

Box containing relics of Pope St Clement in Wardour Castle. Photograph by the author, by courtesy of Lord Talbot of Malahide.

hair. These were obviously relics but not the right ones. On the other side was a similar cabinet, equally difficult to open. It contained a large box covered in red silk with red ribbons fixed in place with wax seals. This must be the 'small box in crimson silk containing relics of a holy martyr', mentioned in Thorpe's 1784 memo.

Eventually the cabinet was opened and I lifted out the heavy box. It measured 24ins x 12ins x 10ins. This was the moment every researcher dreams of – I was carrying the bones of Pope St Clement, a saint who was the third successor of St Peter as Bishop of Rome and who knew personally some of the apostles. 'He had the preaching of the apostles still echoing in his ears.' Lord Talbot sent the sacristan to the vestry again to collect a pile of parchments, many bearing seals. We matched the seals on the box with those on one particular document. It was a letter of authentication signed on 12 December 1791 by Bishop Walmesley. He gave the story of the relics: that they were given by Pope Clement XIII to Lord Arundell on 1 July 1760; they consisted of the holy body and an ampule of the blood of St Clement the Martyr; and that they were placed in a wooden box covered with red silk cloth, tied with red ribbon, well shut and marked with the Pope's small seal. Eureka!

Barry Williamson spent his childhood in a village on the edge of the Wardour estate. He taught History for many years.

Bibliography

Carretta, Vincent, 1990, *George III and the Satirists*, Georgia University

Cannon, J, 1984, *Aristocratic Century, the Peerage of 18th century England*, CUP

Hibbert, Christopher, 1958, *King Mob*, Longmans

Ingamells, John, 1997, *Dictionary of British and Irish Travellers in Italy*, Yale

Jauregui, Maria, & Wilcox, Scott, 2012, *The English Prize*, Yale

Matthew, H G C, & Harrison, Brian (eds), *The Oxford Dictionary of National Biography*, 2004, OUP

Williams, J A, 1968, *Catholic Recusancy in Wiltshire*, Catholic Record Society

Williams, Neville, 1966, *Chronology of the Modern World*, Barrie and Rockliff

Williamson, Barry, 2011, *The Arundells of Wardour*, Hobnob Press

Notes

1 WSA 2667/20/22/1-12, letters from Father Thorpe to the 8th Lord Arundell, 1768-1791

2 At the Ashmolean Museum Oxford, 17 May-27 August 2012 and at the Yale Center for British Art, New Haven, 4 October 2012 -13 January 2013

3 Real Academia de Bellas Artes de San Fernando, Archivo Bibliotecca, 4-87-1-26

4 The Paul Mellon Centre for Studies in British Art. 16 Bedford Square, London WC1B 3JA

5 WSA 2667/20/22/2, November 1770

6 WSA 2667/20/22/4, November 1776

7 WSA 2667/20/22/11, July 1778

8 WSA 2667/20/22/5, July 1778

9 Prince Abbondio Rezzonico (1742-1810), nephew of Pope Clement XIII, Roman Senator and Anglophil

10 WSA 2667/20/22/6, April 1788

11 WSA 2667/20/22/6, May 1788

12 WSA 2667/20/22/6, April 1789

13 It was said to be the largest Catholic community outside London.

14 WSA 2667/20/22/3, February 1774

15 An Heroic Epistle to an Unfortunate Monarch, London 1779, British Museum; Carretta, p233

16 British Museum 5680; Carretta, p238

The Ruins of Fonthill Abbey, John Buckler, 1825

Round about a great estate: the Morrisons at Fonthill since 1829

Caroline Dakers

The Morrison family have owned land at Fonthill for longer than anyone else, including the Grosvenors and their descendants the Shaw-Stewarts, the Beckfords, the Cottingtons and the Mervyns. The wealthy textile merchant James Morrison (1789-1857) began negotiations in 1829 to buy the Fonthill Park Estate from George Mortimer;[1] it is now the property of his great-great-great-grandson Alastair, 3rd Baron Margadale.

This paper is a shortened version of my talk, the second annual *Sarum Chronicle* lecture, given at Salisbury Museum in November 2012. Here I have concentrated on the impact of the Morrisons at Fonthill since 1829, with the emphasis on additions to the estate and the erection, alteration or demolition of buildings.

The *Fonthill Park Estate Particulars* of 1829, now in the Morrison archives,[2] describe a high status estate: 'The high renown which this property has acquired, and the early associations are connected with this almost sacred, and certainly classic ground ... If Elysium can be contemplated upon earth, the claims of Fonthill will be irresistible.' It was particularly attractive to the self-made James Morrison. He was born the son of a prosperous innkeeper in Middle Wallop, a few miles north-east of Salisbury, so knew Fonthill and the stories surrounding the notorious William Beckford and his ill-fated Abbey.[3]

The Park Estate was only part of the original estate owned by Beckford. In 1823 he had moved to Bath after selling all his land including the Abbey to John Farquhar, who had made a fortune dealing in gunpowder in Bengal. After the Abbey collapsed in 1825 Farquhar divided the property, and made arrangements to sell the Abbey Estate to John Benett of Pythouse for £89,416 and the Park Estate to his nephew George Mortimer. Farquhar's death in 1826, before the sales were completed, complicated the situation as his several nieces and nephews became claimants. And the death of Mortimer in 1832 made matters worse. The final settlement of the properties was not made until 1838, although Morrison had taken possession and begun an extensive programme of improvements from 1831 (Benett also made alterations to the Abbey). Morrison paid £35,000, about £3,500,000 in current values. He does not appear to have coveted the ruins of the Abbey. Indeed, as the particulars pointed out, Morrison acquired a picturesque view of the ruins without being responsible for their upkeep: 'The enormous expense connected with the Abbey is now avoided, still retaining all the advantage consequent upon the view of that venerable ruin.'

By 1832 Morrison and his family had taken up residence in the Pavilion, the surviving wing of Alderman Beckford's magnificent mansion Fonthill Splendens. 'It partakes of the style of an Italian Villa, erected of stone, and full of comfort.'[4] Morrison's wife Mary Ann referred to the Pavilion as a 'cottage' though it eventually had 26 rooms. No expense was spared on the decorations, there were painted ceilings, lavish fittings and furnishings (the green and gold curtains in the drawing room cost over £200 (about £20,000 in current values). The site was close up against the wooded slope to the west of the Fonthill cricket field; a new dwelling has just been created within the remains of one of the outbuildings and is visible from the road beside the lake.

Morrison also acquired a woollen factory. This was situated below the weir at the southern end of the lake. The estate particulars described it as 'a freehold clothing establishment … considered to be one of the most compact and valuable Clothing Establishments in the Kingdom.' It was extensive. There was a six-bedroom house with garden and orchard, 24 cottages, a mill of six storeys, 105 feet x 35 feet, containing 'Three Water Wheels, Gear Work, &c. Stocks, Washers,

The Pavilion, engraving, 1829, Morrison archive

Morrisons at Fonthill

The site of cloth factory and cottages, Fonthill Lake, photograph by Caroline Dakers

Indigo Pots, Gigs, Cutters, Carding Machines, Scribbling Machines, Abb-Mules, Warp-Mules, Billies, Brushers, &c.' The wash house was two storeys high, the dye house 136 feet x 14 feet with 'a Steam Boiler, Pipes, &c. Vats, heated by Steam, Furnaces, &c.&c.' There was a Handle House, a Drying House, a Press Room, Store Rooms, Weaving Rooms five storeys and 172 feet long 'containing Stove, Racks, presses, Broad and Narrow Looms, Warping Bars, &c.' It was described rather differently by Morrison's neighbours Lord Arundell and Sir Richard Colt Hoare who commented in their *History of Modern Wiltshire* (1829) on the 'fine transparent lake, disfigured by an unseemly cloth manufactory erected on its banks.'[5]

Morrison had no reason to keep the establishment; his fortune was based on the wholesale trade of textiles from London. Anyway it had ceased operations before he arrived, the 200 workers had sought work elsewhere and the cottages were abandoned. Trees were planted to hide the buildings from the Pavilion and the entire enterprise was gradually dismantled. Morrison's brother, Samuel, came over from Middle Wallop and selected 'some doors, windows, partitions, &c, in the interior of the factory, which he intends to take away.'[6] The factory buildings were of stone but all that now remains are a few walls and suggestive undulations in the grass either side of the stream below the weir. However the water power is

J B Papworth's landing stage, Fonthill Lake, photograph by Caroline Dakers

undiminished and provides electricity for the estate.

Morrison engaged the architect John Buonarotti Papworth to extend the Pavilion, to design new cottages and to improve the pleasure grounds originally laid out by the Beckfords. 'His attention was ... principally devoted to the improvement of the extensive grounds, including plantations, new roads, the bridge at the head of the lake, the quarry gardens, etc., entrances, lodges, gates, lamps, garden pedestals, and vases; seats, and other embellishments.'[7] Beckford's grottos had become overgrown and damaged and repairs were carried out under Papworth's guidance and the management of Morrison's local land agent James Combes. A long passageway, lit at intervals by round spyholes, went under the public road and opened out into a wooded dell above the lake. The tunnel is now closed, however the cromlech is accessible, picturesquely smothered in ivy.

Papworth created a new waterfall at the north end of the lake which could be seen from the Pavilion (to the east of the gatehouse). Combes tried to claim responsibility for the idea when he wrote to Morrison: 'Mr P is much pleasd with the new waterfall and so in fact is every one that has seen it this I always told you would be a great improvement, and the effect produced is quite as good as I anticipated – The view from the House northward is totally changed, I never saw a greater difference in a landscape.'[8] The Morrison children were provided with a number of boats designed by Papworth, including the *Lucy of Fonthill* (named after one of the girls) which they sailed on the lake. The estate particulars were lyrical about the 'the splendid Lake, which it will hardly be accounted treason to denominate the minor Lake of Geneva' ... 'a noble sheet of water, ornamented by lofty and luxuriant banks, abundant in rare fish, and the safe haunt of multitudes of wild fowl, who have long peopled this tranquil and undisturbed region.' There was no bridge (there is now) and Papworth created a grand landing stage on the east side, complete with large stone spheres on pedestals, which is still visible from the public path.

A magnificent gatehouse forms the northern entrance to the estate. The 19th century view, repeated in the estate particulars, supposed it was designed in the 1630s by Inigo Jones: 'its simplicity and proportions display that classic taste with which the distinguished Architect was so familiar.' However more recent architectural historians are unconvinced, preferring a date from the mid-18th century possibly when Alderman Beckford engaged Mr Hoare to build Fonthill Splendens. The main road to Salisbury and London (now 'down-sized' to the minor road connecting Hindon and Dinton) passed conveniently along the north side of the estate, coaches stopping close to the gatehouse. The journey to London still took 12 hours so the arrival of the South Western Railway in Tisbury in 1859-60 made a considerable improvement to communications.

At the southern entrance to the estate Papworth designed a new lodge cottage,

The South Lodge, Fonthill, photograph by Caroline Dakers

J B Papworth's school, Fonthill Bishop, photograph by Caroline Dakers

immediately opposite the Beckford Arms. He also designed a Keeper's Cottage across the lake on Little Ridge (it is close to the present Fonthill House). One of Morrison's tenant farmers commented: 'We all admire the Place thinking it will be a very pretty Cottage in my opinion & the spot that Mr Papworth look out will be a nice one for the House.' He also wondered as 'it is 17 yards long from the Steep of the Hill, where the House is to be built, to the road, wont you want a portion of this Length of Ground for a yard behind the House as well as a Flower Garden in Front.'[9] Papworth designed a Gardener's Cottage inside the ten acre walled garden. Here the 'Hot and Succession Houses, erected on the best principle, are about 220 feet long, the Vines are trembling beneath the abundance of the fruit, and commendation has long since exhausted itself in the attempt to panegyrise sufficiently these far-famed gardens.' While the wall survives, the glass houses have gone and the cottage has been transformed into a large house, just visible to the north of the road leading from the cricket field to Stop Street.

Morrison obtained a government grant towards the erection of a school at Fonthill Bishop. Papworth produced a number of plans in 1838, 'on as economic principle as may be desirable.' He explained: 'The School Room is designed to have a parochial character; as the site is proposed to be the Green, near the Church, it will combine with its style, in perhaps a sufficient degree. As the spot is at the junction of crossing roads, it will be an object seen on every face; perhaps if the corners of the building be placed to the Cardinal points or near to them it will become more picturesquely ornamental, than in any other way, and it is desirable that the sun in its course should visit every face of the building for the benefit of warmth and ventilation.'[10] Both James and Mary Ann Morrison supported the school, paying for heating, books, working materials and clothing. The first schoolteacher, Miss Lucas, was paid £5 10s a quarter. She began work in rented accommodation, and her life was not easy. She wrote to Mary Ann on 19 March 1835: 'I trust you will pardon the liberty I now take in thus addressing you but thinking you would be pleased to see how the Children are getting on with their knitting I have sent you a pr of Garters which I beg you to accept as a small token of gratitude for your very great kindness to me during my illness ... I am very sorry to say that the Shirts are not finished scarce any of the great Girls has been at School lately the two best workers has left the School altogether and the other girls I cannot get to attend sometimes once a week.' Papworth also designed a new church, All Saints, at Chicklade, in 1832. The rector was John Still, also rector of Fonthill Gifford, so it would seem likely Morrison initiated the commission.

Morrison not only improved his property with building, he also extended it, buying the 657 acre Place Farm from his neighbour, Baron Arundell of Wardour. James Everard, 10th Lord Arundell had inherited the Wardour estate in 1817 but his attempts to bring financial order to the property only ended in bankruptcy and he left for Rome where he died in 1834. Place Farm, with its enormous longbarn (200 feet (61 metres) in length) and 14th century farmhouse had been a country retreat of the Abbess of Shaftesbury; it was acquired by the Arundells in 1541. The 10th Lord Arundell first contemplated selling the farm in 1827 but it was his brother Henry, who became the 11th Lord Arundell, who completed the sale to Morrison.[11]

Not content with Place Farm, Morrison also bought Berwick St Leonard, an estate of 1460 acres adjoining the north side of Fonthill, from the Grosvenor family. The Grosvenors (their principal estates were at Eaton in Cheshire and London's west end) had been established in the area since 1821 when Robert Grosvenor, the 1st Marquess, bought Shaftesbury. The Motcombe estate followed in 1825, and Berwick St Leonard in 1826. Neither side could agree the value of Berwick so the case had to go through Chancery; Morrison eventually paid nearly £39,000 in 1844-5. His Fonthill estate thus totalled 3254 acres. He never took the opportunity to buy the Abbey estate. By the time John Benett was keen to sell Morrison had acquired another much larger estate at Basildon in Berkshire and was investing large sums in North America. Richard Grosvenor 2nd Marquess of Westminster bought it from Benett in 1844 for £89,500 (the

Fonthill House c1885. The Morrison archives

same amount Benett had agreed to pay Farquhar's heirs). He demolished most of the ruins as his intention was to build a new house on the site, however he changed his mind and commissioned William Burn to design a new Fonthill Abbey in the 'Scottish Baronial' style about 550 yards (500 metres) away.

Morrison was survived by six sons. His eldest, Charles, inherited Basildon and Islay, Frank took up farming (briefly) at Hole Park in Kent, Walter inherited Malham in Yorkshire, Allan acquired the Hall Barn estate, near Beaconsfield and George purchased Hamptworth in the New Forest. His second son Alfred inherited the Fonthill estate.

The Pavilion had already been enlarged in c1846 by the architect David Brandon (he had designed Wilton Church with T H Wyatt) and Alfred renamed it Fonthill House. The transformation cost £8,000: a tower was added, a portico, a morning room, a conservatory and new servants' wing. After his father's death Alfred carried out further alterations to the interior, largely to accommodate his growing collection of Chinese porcelain, engravings, paintings, furniture, lace, autograph letters and *objets d'art*. He became one of the most important collectors in the second half of the 19th century. Owen Jones, famous as Director of Decorations for the Crystal Palace, was engaged on the first stage, decorating staircases and designing dining-room fittings in ebony and ivory. Three large galleries were added around 1890.

Just like his father, Alfred invested in his estate, extending and building. Unlike his father, however, he inherited a fortune and had no interest in making more money. His brother Charles had noted 'I do not think he will become a working man of business ... nothing but necessity will induce him to become the inmate of a countinghouse [with its] botheration & confinement ...Alfred does not value money, & does like his ease.'[12] He bought additional land almost every year from 1857 to his death in 1897, including part of the manor of Chicklade in 1867–8 and 2205 acres of Great Ridge in 1870. He built his wife Mabel a luxurious wooden cabin on the downs under Great Ridge Wood at a cost of £3000.

Alfred's *aide memoire* opens in 1857 with details relating to the estate: buying sheep feed, attending the assizes at Devizes, the addresses of a local cattle dealer, blacksmith, coach builder, brickmaker and horse breaker. He noted among his London addresses the specialist agricultural book shop in St Martin's lane. And at the back he noted details of taxes, the poor rates and the cost of a seat in church; he also listed the names of the local farmers and clergy with their annual gifts of pheasants, hares and rabbits. He was competitive, applying the same determination to own the 'best' to his art collecting and his country pursuits, breeding prize-winning sheep and horses. His wife Mabel preferred exotic breeds of dogs, keeping borzois, dachshunds, chows, Afghans and a black poodle.

Many of his estate improvements survive. He built two pairs of semi-detached cottages in Stop Street in 1857, identifiable by his elaborately entwined initials AM which he liked to put on most of his possessions including tables, cupboards and books. He 'rebuilt' Berwick St Leonard's church in 1860, also a carpenter's shop and the stone bridge connecting Berwick Farm to the main road. 'Johnnie's Bridge' was named after the estate manager John Read who lived in the

Cottage by Devey, Hindon Lane, Fonthill Gifford. The Morrison archives

farmhouse in the late 19th century.[13] The name of the architect George Devey has been linked to the small thatched cottage built in 1862 on Hindon Lane. But was Devey also responsible for the unusual terrace of four cottages on the Salisbury Road completed in 1864? He was certainly at Fonthill in 1866 as his name and address are entered in Alfred's aide memoire and he possibly oversaw the extensive building work to the gatehouse, including the addition of the walls and ornamental piers on the north side, costing a total of £3327 6s 4d.

In 1864 the Grosvenors commissioned T H Wyatt to design a new church at Fonthill Gifford, Holy Trinity. Alfred's competitive streak was stimulated and in 1879 he paid T H Wyatt to carry out a complete restoration of Fonthill Bishop's Church of All Saints. He also paid for a new font and pulpit for Fonthill Gifford where he was buried in 1897. Mabel paid for a new vestry as a memorial.

Hugh was the eldest son of Alfred and Mabel Morrison. He was the first of the Morrisons to marry into the aristocracy and the first to leave the Liberal party for the Conservatives. Lady Mary Leveson-Gower, whom he married in 1892, was the daughter of the 2nd Earl of Granville; her parents had a house in London virtually next door to the Morrisons. Her grand-father Walter Campbell had sold Islay to James Morrison, and she was related to Lady Elizabeth Grosvenor who lived at the new Fonthill Abbey. The first years of their marriage were troubled by Mary's failure to become pregnant and provide a male heir for Fonthill, and Alfred's failure to write a new will after the birth of his children. His widow Mabel, who was 26 years younger, was left Fonthill House, a large part of his collection (the 'heirlooms') and 300 acres of the estate for her life-time, so Hugh decided in 1902 to commission a new house across the lake on Little Ridge.

He engaged the Arts and Crafts architect Detmar Blow who started by moving the manor house of Berwick St Leonard to the chosen site on Little Ridge. It was

Labourers' cottages, Salisbury Road, Fonthill Bishop, photograph by Caroline Dakers

Morrisons at Fonthill

Construction of walls and piers at the Fonthill gatehouse, c1866. The Morrison archives

an early 17th century house, briefly famous for housing William of Orange on his way to London in 1688. By the 1820s, however, it was being used as a barn so Blow decided to use it to form the centre of the new house. Hugh explained to his land agent Mr Squarey (of Rawlence and Squarey) that this first stage would not exceed £4000. 'I have just seen Blow & have settled to rebuild old Manor House on the site I chose with you on March 22nd at a cost not exceeding £4000 ... so much has been spent at Fonthill last 2 years that I do not consider from what you told me the other day any extensive repairs will be necessary during the coming 12 or 15 months, and except for absolutely necessary repairs I wish <u>all</u> my men to work exclusively for me [on the house].' He asked Squarey's opinion 'whether it would be cheaper to employ traction or whether it would be better either to buy cars and horses using 2 of my own woodmen as carters or to hire carts and horses, you will also consider whether use of traction power would damage the road.'[14]

After 14 years of uncomfortable, sometimes painful 'treatment' for Hugh and Mary, a son, John Granville, was born in 1906. Employees on the Fonthill estate apparently believed Mary only conceived after Hugh was circumcised. The happy couple immediately decided to extend Little Ridge. Then, four years later, Mabel chose to move out of the old Fonthill House (the Pavilion) giving it and her part of the estate to Hugh. She claimed she had never liked the house: 'I hope with all my heart you will pull the house I live in down.' Her wish was almost granted as fire broke out in the empty house in April 1915. The *Salisbury and Winchester Journal* reported the event on 3 April: 'the fire was discovered about half-past three in the morning, and the occupants of the house having been aroused Mr Morrison's chauffeur was dispatched to Tisbury with a motor car to bring back the members of the Tisbury Fire Brigade ... on the arrival of eight members of the Tisbury Brigade under the Captain (Mr George Lush) and the Sub-Captain (Mr Arthur Hibberd) [the hydrants installed in the house] were at once requisitioned.' Water was pumped from the lake. The fire had started in the servants' quarters, in the hot-water apparatus beneath the linen room. A number of paintings and valuable books were carried out on to the lawn and the damage was limited to the servants' quarters. However the decision was taken in 1921 to demolish the house.

Hugh, like his father and grandfather, built new cottages, including several along the Salisbury Road. He was also interested in improving the leisure facilities for his tenants. The late Reg Harris recalled the sports club. There were 'four courts laid out in front of the remains of the old Fonthill House in the Park ... here a pensioner kept the courts mown and marked out ... balls were provided, and even racquits for people who did not have one, all for the princely sum of

Little Ridge House by Detmar Blow. The Morrison archives.

The demolition of Fonthill House, 1921. The Morrison archives.

half a crown a year, this also included membership of the cricket section of the Club, again bats balls pads and stumps were provided. The Morrisons must have donated most of the money I should think.'[15] The cricket field survives to this day, as does the Reading Room, erected in Fonthill Bishop close to the school and church and now used for lectures. It was 'run as a mens club. Here we had a blazing coal fire, a daily newspaper, darts, cards, and the biggest attraction of all a three quarters size billiard table.'[16]

For the Morrisons, life during the first half of the 20th century was luxurious. Part of the fortune made by James Morrison (he died the richest commoner in the 19th century) had passed down through Alfred to Hugh but his wealth was considerably enhanced by legacies from his bachelor uncles Walter and Charles, including large sums of money, investments and most of the island of Islay. Detmar Blow was commissioned to add a very large wing to Islay House and design a house in London's Belgravia, now the Caledonian Club. Hugh was also, through his aristocratic marriage, more socially at ease than his father, and in 1926 he applied for a Patent of Armorial Bearings and Badge showing descent from George Morrison of Nether Wallop. It was, however, his son John who finally received an hereditary title.

John Granville Morrison was made a baron by Sir Alec Douglas Home in 1964 for services to the Conservative party. He had been MP for Salisbury and Chairman of the 1922 Committee, also Master of the South and West Wiltshire Hunt and Senior Steward of the Jockey Club. He married Marjorie Smith, daughter of Lord Hambledon, descendant of W H Smith, another 19th century family made rich through trade.

John Granville had inherited Fonthill in 1931. During the war American soldiers (the 55th Armoured Infantry Battalion of the 11th Armoured Division of General Patton's Third US Army, the 'Thunderbolts') occupied Nissen huts in the park while the British Expeditionary Force evacuated from Dunkirk re-mustered in the park as an armoured division. The Grosvenors' 'new' Fonthill Abbey, which had passed to the Shaw-Stewarts, was requisitioned by the army and knocked about a bit, then sold in 1948 to pay for death duties. John Granville

John Granville Morrison, 1st Baron Margadale, his wife and four children. The Morrison archives

Fonthill Abbey shortly before demolition. The Morrison archives

snapped it up with the intention that it would be a family home for his eldest son James (to become the 2nd Baron Margadale) when he married Clare Barclay. To the relief of James and Clare, who thought it hideous, it was found to have major structural problems, so it was demolished in 1955. It was a fate common to country houses across the whole of Britain, literally hundreds being demolished in the post-war period; many were from the unloved Victorian period. But the much-reduced ruins of Beckford's Abbey remained virtually untouched, hidden within the estate still owned by the Shaw-Stewart family.

For all his inherited wealth, John Granville was engulfed in the 1960s by the demands of Super-tax and property tax, the spiralling costs of maintaining a country house and the poor returns from agricultural land. He shared a common conviction that country house living on large estates had come to an end. Taxes would never be reduced. Investment in agriculture was lost money. He sold the London house and Islay House, he closed down the family's estate office in London, sold many of the 'heirlooms' amassed by Alfred Morrison, and then, in 1972, took the controversial decision to demolish Little Ridge and build a manageable family home within the site. Down-sizing is the term we would now use; the architect Trenwith Wills delivered a 'modest' neo-Georgian house on the

Fonthill House in 2012, photograph by Caroline Dakers

same site incorporating Blow's gardens and a part of the kitchen range. Blow's house had not been listed and a last-minute attempt to get a preservation order failed, apparently because the inspector was sent to the site of the old Fonthill House (the Pavilion) down by the lake. Lord Margadale's obituary in *The Times*, 29 May 1996, quoted him saying 'I can't help it if a government department gets the wrong house.'

Edith Olivier, a close friend of Mabel Morrison, wrote that 'architecture at Fonthill is catastrophic, and houses there live adventurous lives.'[17] 'Fonthill Houses are almost as itinerant as gypsy caravans, although the two resemble each other in no other way. Fonthill is said to have been a "Baronial Seat from the time of the Conquest", but the search for the house in the intervening centuries will find it again and again in a fresh situation.'[18] For the present, however, the 3rd Lord Margadale appears satisfied with the Fonthill House built by his grandfather, although even he could not resist some additions and alterations.

Caroline Dakers is Professor of Cultural History, University of Arts London. Her books include Clouds: Biography of a Country House, *(1993), and* A Genius for Money: Business, Art and the Morrisons, *(2011).*

Notes

Morrisons at Fonthill

1 For permission to use the Morrison archives (which remain in a private collection) I would like to thank Alastair, 3rd Lord Margadale, and his family. For further information about the Morrisons see Dakers, Caroline, 2011, *A Genius for Money, Business, Art and the Morrisons*, Yale University Press.

2 Particulars and Conditions of Sale of the Fonthill Estate ... 29 October 1829, the Morrison archives.

3 Abbey tower was completed in 1806 – at a height of 270 feet (over 80 metres) it would have been visible from the turnpike road between Middle Wallop and Salisbury, some 25 miles away. The abolition of the slave trade, falling sugar prices and overspending on Fonthill forced Beckford to sell up in 1822 and move to Bath.

4 The Pavilion had already been turned into a house for George Mortimer by the architect Thomas Stedman Whitwell (1784–1840).

5 *The History of Modern Wiltshire,* London, p27

6 James Combes to James Morrison, 6 July 1832, the Morrison archives.

7 Wyatt Papworth, 1879, *John B Papworth: a brief record of his life and works*, privately printed, p79

8 James Combes to James Morrison, 2 May 1838, the Morrison archives

9 James Lampard to James Morrison, 19 April 1843, the Morrison archives

10 RIBA 104.1 Note by J B Papworth on his design for Fonthill School, Victoria and Albert Museum/ RIBA Drawings Collection.

11 See Williamson, Barry, 2011, *The Arundells of Wardour. From Cornwall to Colditz*, Hobnob Press. The 10th Lord Arundell was financially incompetent but he was a scholar and book collector and contributed to *The History of Modern Wiltshire* (1829) with his friend and neighbour Sir Richard Colt Hoare of Stourhead.

12 Charles to James Morrison, 5 December 1842, the Morrison archives

13 Reg Harris, 'Memoirs', typescript in the Morrison archives, p2

14 Hugh Morrison to Mr Squarey, 29 March 1902, the Morrison archives

15 Reg Harris, p46

16 Reg Harris, p45

17 Olivier, Edith, 1945, *Four Victorian Ladies of Wiltshire*, Faber, p46

18 Olivier, Edith, 1951, *Wiltshire*, Hale, p296

The Salisbury Domesday Books: a follow up

Steven Hobbs

Issue 12 of *Sarum Chronicle* (2012) included an article that John Chandler and I wrote on the Salisbury City Domesday Books which suggested that these registers of deeds and wills were a comprehensive record of property ownership and transfer from mid–14th to mid–15th centuries and as such an important historical resource.

Several months ago Tom Graham of Corpus Christi College, Oxford, was in the Wiltshire & Swindon History Centre researching the relationship between the bishops of Salisbury and the city. By chance John Chandler was at the History Centre at the same time and they had a useful discussion. Towards the end of his stay Tom came across the following agreement in the City Ledger Book B that makes a valuable footnote to our piece in *Sarum Chronicle*:

> 'An agreement made 14 July 1459, that all deeds and wills are to be entered into the 'Domysday' book by the mayor's clerk back to the year 1441–2. If they are not enrolled the mayor is not to receive his fee and the deeds are deemed to have no title'.

Such fierce retribution for non–compliance indicates the level of comprehensiveness of the books and thus their significance.

From Medieval Catholic Piety to Civil War Protestantism: the Impact of the Reformation in Two Salisbury Parishes

Claire Cross

With its great cathedral, multiplicity of clergy and flourishing parish churches Salisbury in the early 16th century could well be seen as an exemplar of late medieval English Catholicism, yet within one or at the most two generations the majority of its leading citizens had moved from entrenched conservatism to advanced Protestantism. By drawing on contemporary evidence – very occasional letters, an exceptional diary, the laconic and intermittent churchwardens' accounts, a handful of printed sermons and well in excess of 700 surviving wills – this paper attempts to trace this transition in religious belief in the two central parishes of St Thomas's and St Edmund's.[1]

Unlike most English cathedral cities, which if not of Roman origin could at the very least trace their foundation back to the early middle ages, Salisbury owed its existence to Bishop Richard Poore, who early in the reign of Henry III transplanted his cathedral and township of Old Sarum from a wind–swept hill top to the much more hospitable water meadows of the river Avon. The building of the new cathedral began in 1220 and the town with its celebrated grid pattern was laid out at precisely the same time. The bishop seems to have had no difficulty in attracting tenants to take up his burgage plots and New Sarum very soon gained all the outward attributes of a thriving urban centre. The office of mayor had emerged as early as 1249 and by the next century the government of the town was in the hands of an annually elected mayor and 24 councillors. In 1406 the crown granted this body the right to acquire and hold land in perpetuity, but it still remained an episcopal borough. Every year the mayor had to swear his oath of office before one of the bishop's servants and the citizens had to sue in the bishop's court. The struggle for emancipation from episcopal control lasted for almost 400 years and the city only obtained its royal charter of incorporation in 1612.[2]

Unlike older cathedral cities which tended to have a large number of small parishes, up to the Victorian era Salisbury had a mere three, St Martin's, St Thomas's and St Edmund's. St Martin's church, which largely served the hamlet outside the ramparts, predated New Sarum by several centuries. The new city had only one church dedicated to St Thomas of Canterbury England's recently martyred archbishop until 1269, when Bishop Walter de la Wyle divided the parish into two to create the collegiate church of St Edmund of Abingdon. Largely dependent on the cloth industry Salisbury grew rapidly in the late middle ages, and by the early 16th century St Thomas's and St Edmund's were each said to have had over a thousand communicants.[3]

By this date the parishes possessed two fine parish churches. St Edmund's, a cruciform building with a central tower and spire, had undergone considerable enlargement around 1400 with the nave, which functioned as the parish church, extended to 78 feet in length. Much reconstruction had also taken place at St Thomas's after the collapse of the chancel roof in 1447 when the wealthy merchant, William Swayne, had rebuilt the south chancel aisle. The interiors of the two churches were equally splendid. Both had a series of wall paintings, with those in St Thomas's depicting the Annunciation, the Visitation and the Adoration of the Shepherds in the Swayne chapel, and the Last Judgement over the chancel arch. The churches were also filled with painted glass, now all lost, though windows in St Thomas's are known to have contained a Tree of Jesse and scenes from Genesis and the Assumption of the Virgin and one window in St Edmund's to have portrayed God in the act of creating the world. The Tailors' Guild, St George's Guild, and some lesser guilds maintained altars and priests in St Thomas's; the Weavers' Guild and other guilds had their altars and priests in St Edmund's.[4]

Neither parish had its own rector or vicar, with the dean and chapter of the cathedral, which had acquired the advowson from the bishop of Salisbury in 1399, merely appointing a curate to officiate at St Thomas's, and the priests of St Edmund's College ministering in both the parishes of St Edmund's and St Martin's. There were 11 priests in addition to the provost and nine canons in St Edmund's in 1380, and no fewer than 26 chaplains and 11 unbeneficed clergy in St Thomas's at the same date. Because of their demand for prayers for the dead the laity seem to have been largely responsible for this very large number of clergy. Seven permanent chantries each with its individual priest had been founded in

Medieval wall painting of Mary and Elizabeth, Lady Chapel, St Thomas's church. Photograph by Chris Broadhurst.

St Edmund's over the course of the middle ages and at least four in St Thomas's. Those unable to afford the very considerable expense of a permanent chantry could arrange for a priest to pray for their souls for a certain number of years.[5]

Throughout the early Tudor period parishioners continued to employ priests in this way. In 1517, for example, in addition to covering the roof of St John the Baptist's aisle in St Edmund's with lead John Selwode bequeathed two houses and gardens to the Jesus Guild for its priest to pray in perpetuity for the souls of himself, his family, benefactors and friends. Five years later the mercer, Thomas Coke, left 200 marks (£133 6s 8d) for an honest secular priest to say mass daily for his soul and the souls of his parents, brothers and sisters, and all the faithful departed in St Thomas's for 20 years. In 1530 another mercer, Henry Acton, gave

North West view of church, detail from *A Plan of St. Thomas Church, taken by John Lyon,* 1745, in Swayne's *Churchwarden's Accounts.*

St Edmund's £16 for the purchase of two service books and hired a priest for six years to pray for his soul and the souls of his mother and father, while as late as 1536 Mercy Byrkhead could make provision for a priest to sing and pray for her soul and all Christian souls for four years.[6]

While several burnings of heretics had taken place in Salisbury between 1502 and 1520 these Lollards had originated from elsewhere in the diocese and there is no record of any religious dissent in the city itself. The inhabitants in consequence seem to have been totally unprepared for the Act of Supremacy of 1534 which recognised Henry VIII and not the pope as the head of the English church. For a decade the bishopric of Salisbury had been held *in absentia* by the papal diplomat, Lorenzo Campeggio. In 1534 he was deprived of his see by another Act of Parliament and early in the following year the crown appointed as his successor Nicholas Shaxton, an advanced evangelical and almoner to Anne Boleyn. The moment he arrived in the city accompanied by his even more outspoken Scottish chaplain, John MacDowell, Shaxton started attacking traditional religious practices and promoting the reading of the newly translated English Bible.[7]

A confrontation between a radical bishop and a religiously conservative city seemed almost inevitable, and battle commenced early in 1536 on the council's failure to punish certain townspeople who had torn down licences relaxing fasting in Lent. This led MacDowell in a Passion Sunday sermon in St Edmund's to question the city governors' support for the royal supremacy, and in a letter to Shaxton to charge them with ignoring the king's commissions, retaining the bishop of Rome's name in their mass books and still displaying papal pardons. The council responded by imprisoning MacDowell for slander.[8]

Things now descended into a slanging match with the bishop and his chaplain denouncing the townspeople as crypto–papists, and the mayor and his supporters inveighing against Shaxton and MacDowell as dangerous sacramentaries who denied the miracle of the mass. The mayor and councillors then made a new attempt to free themselves from episcopal control, petitioning Thomas Cromwell to 'qualify' the 15th century charter which had confirmed the bishop's lordship over the city. Shaxton retaliated by informing the king's chief minister that Thomas Chaffyn, a member of the twenty–four and a leading parishioner of St Thomas's, had been asserting that 'the city is the king's city, the mayor is the king's mayor and the king's lieutenant', when Edward IV's charter made it abundantly plain that 'the city is the bishop's city, the citizens the bishop's citizens and the mayor the bishop's mayor...' Even more dangerously, taking their lead from Chaffyn the mob had gone around proclaiming 'the city is the king's etc., the bishop is an heretic, and we trust to see him hanged.'[9]

A year later the bishop's under–bailiff sent Cromwell details of 'the privy practices of certain priests in Sarum who in confession forbid white meats in Lent, the reading of the New Testament in English and the company of those of the new learning.' He exceeded his brief, however, at Easter 1539 when he prevented people from kissing an image which unknown to him contained a consecrated host, and had hastily to explain to Cromwell that he had acted against the abuse of the image and not against the blessed sacrament itself. Then with the controversy still unresolved conservatives gained the upper hand at Westminster. Shaxton resigned his see in protest at the passing of the Act of Six Articles, and his much more diplomatic successor wisely let sleeping dogs lie.[10]

The townspeople meanwhile seem to have done the bare minimum to comply with the religious legislation. The pope no longer figured in their public prayers, the churchwardens of St Edmund's spent 5s on a Bible in 1538/9 and their counterparts at St Thomas's changed their church's dedication from the now politically unacceptable St Thomas Becket to the ideologically anodyne St Thomas the Apostle. Yet, notwithstanding the attacks upon the doctrine of purgatory and the worship of the saints, priests were celebrating masses for the dead, the wives, the young people and the servants were raising funds to keep the lights burning before the images and the churches' vestments, ornaments and banners were being regularly repaired much as they had been before the break with Rome.[11]

Everything changed on the accession of Edward VI when Thomas Hancock took it upon himself to visit the city. An Oxford graduate, Hancock had been suspended from his curacy at Amport near Andover in Hampshire in the latter years of Henry VIII for teaching that Christ had suffered once only for the sins of the whole world. With his preaching licence now restored he seized the opportunity to deliver a sermon in St Thomas's before the chancellors of the bishops of Salisbury and Winchester and other leading members of the clergy and laity. Taking as his text Matthew XV. 13: 'Every plant which my heavenly Father planted not, shall be rooted up', he railed 'against the superstitious ceremonies as holy bread, holy water, images, copes, vestments etc. and at the last against the idol of the altar, proving it to be an idol, and no God, by the first of St John's gospel, ["No man hath seen God at any time." John I. 18.].' Then directly addressing the congregation he observed 'that the priest holdeth over his head you do see, you kneel before it, you honour it and make an idol of it, and you yourselves are most horrible idolaters.'[12]

At this the doctors and other clergy walked out in disgust, and after the service had ended, the mayor, Thomas Chaffyn, accused Hancock of offending against a recent royal proclamation prohibiting criticism of the sacrament of the altar, to which Hancock retorted 'that it was no sacrament, but an idol as they do use it.' Most of those present at the sermon agreed with the mayor that Hancock should be imprisoned, but he retained his liberty when 'six honest men' offered to stand as his sureties. At a subsequent appearance at the Assizes he was bound over for a second time on a bond for £100 for which Harry Dymock, a woollen draper and a member of St Thomas's parish, was one of the guarantors. Having appealed to the Duke of Somerset Hancock was eventually released from his bond but only on condition that he avoided stirring up religious passions in the future.[13]

Whatever their sympathies, the townspeople had little alternative but to go along with the protestant innovations of the reign of Edward VI. In 1547 the St Thomas's churchwardens pulled down the statues of St George and other saints and sold two hundredweight of memorial brasses, in 1550 their counterparts in St Edmund's employed five labourers to dismantle their altars, and both parishes subsequently surrendered most of their costly vestments and ornaments. They bought copies of the first *Book of Common Prayer* and numerous psalm books in 1549, and from this date referred to the communion service rather than the mass. The purchase of the decisively protestant second *Book of Common Prayer* in the autumn of 1552 completed the religious revolution.[14]

Although Hancock had almost certainly exaggerated the extent of his support, the city did contain some convinced Protestants such as John Whelpeley, merchant, who even in Mary's reign trusted to be saved by the merits of Christ alone. Yet these converts seem to have been greatly outnumbered in the Edwardian period by conservatives like the merchant, William Bryan, of St Edmund's, Alice Martin of St Thomas's and the mercer and a former mayor, Christopher Chaffyn, who still all requested prayers for their souls or called upon the intervention of the Virgin Mary and the saints at their deaths.[15]

The traditionalists came into their own when Mary Tudor succeeded her half–brother in July 1553. Almost at once St Edmund's churchwardens restored their altars and re–acquired the Latin service books necessary for the performance of the catholic liturgy. In a will made in January 1554 William Webbe, a former mayor, returned to St Thomas's 'all such vestments as I lately bought by virtue of a commission sent down for the sale of the same by the late King Edward the Sixth', and left the church a rent charge of 20s in perpetuity towards the cost of celebrating the morrow mass and the Jesus mass together with a further 20s a year

Arms of Queen Elizabeth I, St Thomas's church. Photograph by Chris Broadhurst.

for 20 years to the clerks and singing men 'for the maintenance of God's service'. Throughout the reign testators of both parishes habitually commissioned requiem masses and the parishioners of St Thomas's re–adopted St Thomas of Canterbury as their patron saint. In 1557 St Thomas's churchwardens recorded the purchase of incense, processions with banner bearers and cope bearers, collections for the font taper, and the gathering of money by the wives, daughters and servants at Hocktide and the Friday in Whitsun week. To all outward appearances the old religion had triumphed over the new.[16]

The catholic revival ended abruptly on Elizabeth's accession on 17 November 1558. In the following spring Parliament passed fresh Acts of Supremacy and Uniformity and, under the vigilant eye of the new bishop of Salisbury, the former Marian exile and leading anti–catholic controversialist, John Jewel, the townspeople had for the second time to adapt to a protestant regime. The churchwardens of both churches once again destroyed their altars and removed their statues, bought the *Book of Common Prayer*, *The Homilies* and the *Paraphrases* of Erasmus, and St Thomas's changed its dedication back to St Thomas the Apostle. In 1560 St Thomas's paid a painter and his man for 'for writing of scripture in the church' and the next year set up the royal arms over the chancel arch, and a few years later St Edmund's erected two tables containing the Ten Commandments and the Lord's Prayer. In 1567 St Edmund's wardens sold off all the rest of their catholic accoutrements, banners, candlesticks, curtains, a holy water pot, a pyx, banners, and stoles, and around the same time their counterparts at St Thomas's raised £34 by disposing of certain goods belonging to the church, in 1572 converted some albs lying around in the vestry into surplices and a year later sold off some small bells, cruets and a holy water pot. In the now white–washed churches only the stained glass remained as a reminder of the old religion, and some of that was destroyed in St Thomas's in 1583 when the wardens put 'out the picture of [God] the Father in the east window at Mr Subdean's commandment'.[17]

Though the direction for change came from above, some parishioners seem to have actively welcomed the return of Protestantism. As early as January 1562 John Gough, inn holder, made a very protestant profession of faith in his will and set aside 6s 8d for 'a faithful preacher of God's holy word' to deliver his funeral sermon in St Edmund's church. John Webbe, a city councillor and the son of William Webbe who had preserved St Thomas's vestments, opted for a decisively protestant preamble in his will in 1571. Having established a permanent loan scheme for the city's broad loom weavers William Wotton, ale brewer, of St Edmund's in 1572 arranged for a preacher to 'make a sermon' in St Edmund's each year on the day that the money was distributed. After prefacing his will with a personal statement of his protestant beliefs in 1579 William Chambers left Mr Thomas Thackam, the vicar of Bradford on Avon, £10 to preach 20 sermons every year for the next three years 'within Wiltshire in places most needful'. In 1580 John West expressed the hope 'through the merits of Jesus Christ my saviour to enjoy the kingdom of heaven purchased with his most precious blood for his elect.' Having provided 20 shillings for ' three godly sermons' in St Edmund's Christopher Eyre, clothier, in 1582 beseeched God 'to send into his church faithful ministers and sincere preachers of his word and those in number many and in operation wonderful.'[18]

Eyre's prayer was answered in 1617 when his namesake and probable relative the London merchant Christopher Eyre, son of the Salisbury alderman, Thomas Eyre, founded a lectureship in St Thomas's. With an annual income of £20 it was sufficient to attract well qualified university graduates to the city, and its first incumbent, the Calvinist John Davenport, in 1621 went on to become bishop of Salisbury, a post he held throughout the Laudian period until his death 20 years later.[19]

Yet hearing of the Word was not enough, a lively faith needed to manifest itself in good works, and in the early 17th century the corporation embarked on an audacious scheme of civic renewal. The disastrous decline of cloth production since its heyday in the late middle ages had resulted in unprecedented numbers of unemployed and underemployed able bodied poor in the early modern period. Under the guidance of their pastor, John White, the adjacent, though much smaller, county town of Dorchester, had been tackling the problem since 1605 by setting up schools, a workhouse, and a hospital all financed by the profits from the communal brewery, and at some date before 1620 certain influential inhabitants of Salisbury made the decision to follow Dorchester's lead.[20]

The right to present to the living of St Edmund's, which had passed to a lay proprietor at the Reformation, had been temporarily acquired by the parish vestry in 1611. Dominated by the city's recorder, Henry Sherfield, and John Ivie, a prominent goldsmith, in 1623 the vestry offered the vacant living to Peter Thatcher, vicar of Milton Clevedon in Somerset. An Oxford graduate, Thatcher had aligned himself with a circle of Somerset clergy and laity advocating further reform in the church; he was also an admirer of White and kept in contact with him throughout his ministry. On his arrival in Salisbury he threw his support behind the corporation's campaign 'to reform the drunkenness, idleness, running to the alehouse and other such courses, which have been and are the bane of our poor in Sarum'.[21]

Around a third of Salisbury's inhabitants had fallen below the poverty line by the 1620s, and an outbreak of plague in 1627 made a bad situation worse. The mayor, John Ivie, resolved to break the mould 'and to settle a livelihood for the comfortable living of poor souls whereby God may be glorified and our city comforted' by creating a storehouse to sell provisions to the poor at cost price.

Thatcher pronounced the venture to be for 'the public good' of the city and for a while the recently established civic brewery and the storehouse seemed to be succeeding in improving the material conditions of the poor.[22]

Within St Edmund's parish, where some of Thatcher's more affluent parishioners had responded favourably to his ministry from the start, the vestry had decreed early in 1630 that 'Mr Recorder [Henry Sherfield] may, if it please him, take down the window wherein God is painted in many places as if he were there creating the world; so as he do instead thereof new make the same window with white glass ...' Nothing happened for nine months, during which time the bishop of Salisbury issued an injunction inhibiting any precipitate action. This weighed little with Sherfield, who as a Member of Parliament for Salisbury between 1624 and 1629 had joined in the attacks on Buckingham and the Arminians, and even more recently had obtained a confirmation of the city's charter restating its independence from the bishop. Entering the church one night in October armed with a pike staff, he demolished the offensive window, injuring himself in the process. Judged guilty of iconoclasm by the Star Chamber, fined the huge sum of £500 and ordered to make a public confession Sherfield did not live long after his disgrace, dying in January 1634. During the trial Archbishop Laud had also sought to implicate Thatcher, who, he maintained, had 'not read all the divine service in a whole year together.'[23]

Now a marked man, for a while Thatcher considered leaving Salisbury for a safe haven in Herefordshire, where Sir Robert Harley had offered him the living of Brampton Bryan. Resolving finally to stay in the city, he now looked to the new world to redress the evils of the old. In 1635 he sponsored the emigration to Massachusetts of his brother, Anthony, and his own teenage son, Thomas, and lent the settlers £35 to buy livestock. Within Salisbury itself the hostility of the ecclesiastical authorities served only to increase Thatcher's reputation and in both 1636 and 1637 Robert Eyre, junior, his wife, and no fewer than 25 other members of St Thomas's were admonished in the sub–dean's court for frequenting St Edmund's to hear sermons. Other inhabitants shared their minister's vision to create a fully reformed church across the Atlantic and in 1638 Christopher Batt and the surgeon, John Green, were among the 12 local men who founded a new Salisbury in New England, where six years later they were joined by Mr Edmund Batter, the brother of the haberdasher, Richard Allwood. Yet other merchants were fostering links with continental Protestants: in 1637 Anthony Hooper bequeathed £10 to be divided between a Huguenot temple near St Malo and its minister, while Thomas Barfote and his father were forging close ties with the minister of the Reformed church of Pontivy.[24]

Thatcher lived just long enough to see the summoning of the Long Parliament and the eclipse of the Laudians. At his death early in 1641 he bequeathed his library of over a hundred volumes of continental and English protestant theology to his son Thomas, who ended his life as the minister of the Old South church in Boston. Memories of his ministry lingered long in the parish, and as late as 1649 Richard Carter, gentleman, asked to be buried in St Edmund's next to the tomb of his 'late reverend pastor Mr Peter Thatcher'.[25]

Within days of Thatcher's death the vestry offered the living to John Strickland a northerner, who had graduated MA from Oxford in 1625 and spent a year assisting John White in Dorchester before he secured the rectory of Podimore Milton in Somerset in 1632. Chosen as a member of the Westminster Assembly of Divines in the autumn of 1643 Strickland almost immediately began making his influence felt not only on the local but also on the national stage. In an address given before the House of Commons in St Margaret's on 27 December he rejoiced that God had redressed the Romish abuses of the previous decade when 'the Sabbath ...was beaten down from the press and pulpit' and 'men's consciences' were oppressed 'with intolerable burdens'. The following April he exhorted the lord mayor and aldermen of the city of London to execute the 'wholesome laws' recently enacted by Parliament. Then in the autumn of 1644, by which time the Parliamentarians had gained the upper hand over the Royalists, he called upon the House of Lords to promote the Directory of Worship, supervise the taking of the covenant and settle the government of the church. In October 1645 in the last of his published sermons he reminded Parliament yet again of the pressing need to restore 'God's house'.[26]

By this date a cleric of a very similar theological standpoint had joined Strickland in Salisbury. Having been prevented by the cathedral authorities four years previously from appointing as their curate John Conant, a former fellow of Exeter College, Oxford and rector of Limington in Somerset since 1619, St Thomas's vestry took advantage of Parliament's abolition of deans and chapters to secure him for the parish in 1645. Like Strickland Conant sat as a member of the Westminster Assembly of Divines and he, too, had preached before the House of Commons in 1643, when he urged upon magistrates the necessity of executing the recently enacted 'wholesome ordinances'.[27]

Anxious that Strickland might accept a more prestigious post, St Edmund's vestry went to considerable lengths to retain his services, paying for substitutes to supply his 'ministerial function' during his long absences in London, and petitioning Parliament in February 1646 to supplement the living. In 1647 St Martin's appointed William Eyre, a Hebrew scholar and another member of the Westminster Assembly, as their minister and the following year Parliament granted each of the three clerics annual stipends of £150, far more than the parochial clergy had been receiving before the Civil War; they also had the use of one of the four canons' houses in the close recently purchased by the corporation. Pleading

St Edmund's church. From Hall's *Picturesque Memorials of Salisbury* 1834.

with the nation's rulers to imitate 'the righteous sceptre of Christ' in 1652 Eyre preached the assize sermon in St Thomas's church, where he moved permanently as minister on Conant's death in 1653. As committed as ever to promoting 'the kingdom of Jesus Christ, and the prosperity of the commonwealth in which we live', in the 1650s Strickland concentrated much more of his attention upon his Salisbury parish. Both he and Eyre were also very active in the Wiltshire Association in which like minded clergy met together 'for mutual assistance and advice.'[28]

A catastrophe which occurred in St Edmund's in 1653 gives some indication of the sober religious atmosphere which now prevailed in the city. Despite the vestry having undertaken a restoration in 1632, erected buttresses against the north wall in 1638, carried out further repairs in 1643 and 1644, and removed the bell on the top of the tower in 1651, the church still remained in a very fragile state. Summoned to an extraordinary meeting on 19 June 1653 the parish next agreed to take down all the bells except the great bell and the treble bell 'and that this be done with what speed possible that so the south west pillar may be amended.'[29]

This was all too little and too late. On the Sabbath day, 26 June, 'when the mayor and many other principal inhabitants of the city with a great multitude of godly Christians were met at Edmund's church for the public worship of God ... the main pillars did bulge out, and sensibly shake; the clefts in the walls were seen to open and shut with ringing the sermon bell...' In the emergency the parish could find no suitable props to set under the tower, 'so nothing but the very hand of God did keep the stones and timber from falling until the next morning, that his own people were all secured at home, and then He so sweetly ordered the fall of the tower that, albeit many workmen were about it that day, neither man, woman nor child received any hurt thereby.'[30]

To commemorate this providential escape the vestry ordained 'that the twenty–six day of June yearly shall be unto the people of Edmund's parish a day of solemn and public thanksgiving unto God for the same ... And we do farther order that either in the windows or the walls or the gates of our new builded church ... there be made as shall be thought fit some monuments of the late deliverance.[31]

To provide the parish with an alternative place to worship, the vestry next took the decision to demolish the nave, destabilised by the fall of the tower, and refurbish the previously little used chancel, commissioning John Ivie and the merchant Thomas Hancock to oversee the setting up of the pulpit and new seats 'with all convenient speed'. This done they spent much of the following years raising funds for the rebuilding of the tower which they completed by the summer of 1658. With a gallery over the newly constructed great west door, and seats across the bottom of the east window they had transformed St Edmund's into a preaching house, where Sunday by Sunday the parish could once again gather to hear their 'loving pastor, Mr John Strickland'.[32]

The restoration of Charles II brought this godly experiment to an end. In April 1662 one parishioner of St Edmund's voiced his fear that his minister might not be permitted to preach his funeral sermon, and on Strickland's refusal to conform he and William Eyre of St Thomas's were both ejected on St Bartholomew's day the following August. Eyre retired to Melksham but Strickland remained in the city and established a congregation which later in the decade was attracting 200 worshippers. At his death in 1664 John Ivie left a remembrance to 'Mr John Strickland, late minister of our parish'. Strickland himself survived until October 1670, when he bequeathed his polyglot *Bible* and *The Works of St Augustine* to Thomas Roswell and William Gough, his two ministerial sons–in–law, who like him had lost their livings in 1662. In December that year the churchwardens of St Edmund's carried out an injunction to replace the seats under the east window with a communion table, and by the end of the century the bishop had won the right to present to the benefice.[33]

The religious faith of such leaders of the community as John Ivie and Thomas Hancock or of humbler citizens like John Butcher, George Mervyn and Richard Phelps who in the 1650s and 1660s directed their benefactions to the relief of the

Plaque on tower of St Edmund's church. Photograph by Jane Howells 2013.

deserving poor, commissioned funeral sermons and made bequests to civic clergy seems a world away from that of Henry Acton, Joan Peerse, Mercy Byrkhede or John Hawles who throughout the 1530s were still donating expensive service books and vestments to their parish churches and hiring priests to pray for their souls. Hostile as the townspeople may have been to the Reformation innovations of Bishop Shaxton and his chaplain within a generation their magistrates and ministers had committed themselves to Protestantism, and for a time in the next century came near to realising in Salisbury their vision of the city of God.[34]

Claire Cross taught in the History Department of the University of York from which she retired as professor in 2000. Her most recent publications include, co–edited with P S Barnwell and Ann Rycraft, Mass and Parish in Late Medieval England: the use of York *(2005). From 2005 to 2010 she was chairman of the British Association for Local History.*

Abbreviations and Bibliography

ODNB = *Oxford Dictionary of National Biography* 2004
TNA = documents at The National Archives
WAM = *Wiltshire Archaeological and Natural History Magazine*
WSA = documents at the Wiltshire and Swindon History Centre

Apart from book titles the spelling in all quotations has been modernised.

Brown, A D, 1995, *Popular Piety in late Medieval England: the Diocese of Salisbury, 1250–1550,* Oxford University Press
Calamy, E, 1775, *The Nonconformist's Memorial,* ed S Palmer
Chandler, J, 1983, *Endless Street: a History of Salisbury and its People,* Hobnob Press
Crittall, E, (ed), 1962, *The Boroughs of Wilton and Old Salisbury, the City of New Salisbury. Victoria History of the Counties of England: A History of Wiltshire,* volume 6 (*VCH6*), OUP for the Institute of Historical Research
Haskins, C, 1912, *The Ancient Trade Guilds and Companies of Salisbury,* Bennett Bros
Hatcher, H, 1843, *Old and New Sarum or Salisbury,* Nichols. Part of Hoare, C, *History of Modern Wiltshire,* 6 vols 1822–44
Hollaender, A, 1944, The Doom Painting of St Thomas of Canterbury, Salisbury, *WAM,* volume 50, pp351–70
Matthews, A G, 1934, *Calamy Revised,* Clarendon Press
Nichols, J G, (ed), 1859, *Narratives of the Days of the Reformation,* Camden Society, Old Series volume 77
Pugh, R B, and Crittall, E, (eds), 1956, *Victoria History of the Counties of England: A History of Wiltshire,* volume 3 (*VCH3*), OUP for the Institute of Historical Research
Slack, P, (ed), 1975, *Poverty in Early–Stuart Salisbury,* Wiltshire Record Society, volume31
Street, F, 1916, The Relations of the Bishops and Citizens of Salisbury (New Sarum) between 1225 and 1612, *WAM* volume 39
Swayne, H J F, (ed), 1896, *Churchwardens' Accounts of S. Edmund and S. Thomas, Sarum, 1443-1702,* Wilts Record Society
Underdown, D, 1992, *Fire from Heaven. Life in an English Town in the Seventeenth Century,* Harper Collins

Notes

1   The first section of this paper is a condensed version of Cross, Claire, Religious Cultures in Conflict: a Salisbury Parish during the English Reformation, in Dyer, C, Hopper, A, Lord, E and Tringham, N, (eds), 2011, *New Directions in Local History since Hoskins,* University of Hertfordshire Press, pp 159-171 and published here with permission.
2   Street, pp185–257, 319–67; *VCH6*, pp94–7, 101–3
3   *VCH6*, pp69, 79-81, 151-2, 385; Brown, p74; and for a more detailed account of religion in late medieval Salisbury see Chandler, p193-9
4   *VCH6*, pp149, 151-3; Haskins, pp31, 134–9; Hollaender, pp351-70
5   *VCH3*, pp385-9; *VCH6*, pp147–8, 152; Hatcher, pp264–5; Haskins, pp146, 163; Brown, pp137, 139
6   TNA, PROB 11/16 (William Coke), 11/19 (John Selwode), 11/23 (Henry Acton), 11/25 (Mercy Byrkhede)
7   Mayer, T F 'Campeggi [Campeggio], Lorenzo (1471/2-1539), diplomat and bishop of Salisbury', *ODNB*, 9, pp871–2); Wabuda, S, 'Shaxton, Nicholas (c. 1485-1556), bishop of Salisbury', *ODNB*, 50, pp133–6; Durkan, J, 'MacDowell [Maydland, Madwell, Maydwell], John (b. c.1500, d. in or after 1556), Dominican friar and evangelical reformer', *ODNB*, 35, pp 334–5
8   *Letters and Papers of Henry VIII*, 12, pt 1, nos 746, 755, 756, 824, 838 (hereafter *LP Hen VIII)*; Street, pp322–8
9   *LP Hen VIII*, 12, pt. 2, nos 52, 1114
10 *LP Hen VIII*, 13, pt 2, nos 141, 606; 14 pt 1, nos 777, 778; 15, no 498 (57)
11 Swayne, pp72, 84, 86, 273-4
12 Nichols, pp72–3
13 Nichols, pp74–7
14 Swayne, pp75, 90-1, 97, 275–9
15 TNA, PROB 11/32 (William Bryan) 11/34 (Alice Martyn), 11/34 (Christopher Chafyn), 11/37 (John Whelpeley)
16 Swayne, pp99-103, 279; TNA, PROB 11/36 (William Webbe the elder), 11/41 (John Corriatt)
17 Swayne, pp104-5, 111, 115, 143, 280, 281, 282, 285–6, 286-7, 287–8, 290-1, 293–4
18 WSA, P1/2 Reg/130 (John Gough), TNA, PROB 11/53 (John Webbe), 11/55 (William Wotton), 11/61 (William Chambers), 11/55 (John Weste), 11/65 (Christopher Eyer)
19 *VCH6*, pp 149-50
20 Underdown; Slack (1975)
21 *VCH6*, pp151-2; Slack, P 'Thatcher [Thacher], Peter (1587/8-1641), Church of England clergyman', *ODNB*, 54, pp207-8
22 Slack, 'Thatcher, Peter', *ODNB*, 54, pp 207-8; Slack (1975), p7; Ivie, J, 1661, *A Declaration,* sig. A2 [re-printed in Slack (1975)]
23 TNA PROB 11/144 (William Creede), 11/151 (John Vuxton), 11/157 (John Raye); Swayne, p190; Slack, P, 1972, Religious Protest and Urban Authority: the Case of Henry Sherfield, Iconoclast, 1633, *Studies in Church History*, 9, pp 295-302; Slack, P, The Public Conscience of Henry Sherfield, in Morrill, J, Slack, P and Woolf, D, (eds), 1993, *Public Duty and Private Conscience in Seventeenth-Century England,* Clarendon Press, pp167-71; Slack, 'Thatcher, Peter', *ODNB*, 54, pp207-8; Chandler, pp201-2
24 Slack, 'Thatcher, Peter', *ODNB*, 54, pp207-8; Lewin, C G, 2005, Housekeeping in Salisbury, 1640, *Sarum Chronicle* 5, p15; Chandler, J, see below p125 ; TNA PROB 11/187 (Peter Thatcher), 11/178 (William Dawling), 11/192 (Richard Allwood), 11/312 (Anthony Hooper), 11/295 (Thomas Barfote)

25 Slack, 'Thatcher, Peter', *ODNB*, 54, pp207-8; TNA PROB 11/187 (Peter Thatcher), 11/210 (Richard Carter)

26 Swayne, p212; Lancaster, H, 'Strickland, John (bap. 1601?, d. 1670)', *ODNB*, 53, p77; E. Calamy, II, p511; Matthews, pp 467-8; Chandler, p201; Strickland, J, 1644, *Gods work of mercy in Sions Misery*, pp10, 29, 30; Strickland, J, 1644, *A discovery of peace: or, The thoughts of the Almighty for the ending of his peoples calamities*, dedication; Strickland, J,1644, *Immanuel, or The Church Triumphing in God with us*, pp16, 25; Strickland, J, 1645, *Mercy rejoycing against judgement: or God waiting to be gracious to a sinfull nation*, pp18, 23

27 Wallace, D D, jun, 'Conant, John (1608-1694), college head', *ODNB*, 12, pp912-914; *VCH6*, p 150; Conant, John, 1643, *The woe and weale of Gods people displayed in a sermon preached before the honourable House of Commons at their late solemn humiliation on July 26, 1643*, pp33-5

28 Swayne, pp205, 214-15, 221; Matthews, p187; *VCH6*, p119; Eyre, W, 1652, *Christ's scepter advanced, or the righteous administrations of Christ's kingdome set forth for the imitation of earthly rulers in a sermon preached at the assizes holden in the city of New Sarum in the county of Wilts on Saturday the 31 of July 1652*, pA 2; Chambers, H, Bifield, A, Strickland, J and Ince, P, 1654, *An Apology for the Ministers of the County of Wilts, in their Actings at the election of Members for the approaching Parliament In Answer to a Letter sent out of the said County, Pretending to lay open the dangerous Designes of the Clergy, in reference to the approaching Parliament*, pp22-3

29 Swayne, pp 196-7, 203, 208-9, 215, 226, 227; Chandler, pp 203-4

30 Swayne, p228; Chandler, p204

31 Swayne, p228

32 Swayne, pp 228-9, 230-1, 234, 235; TNA PROB 11/282 (Richard Grafton)

33 TNA PROB 11/310 (George Mervyn); 11/322 (John Ivie); 11/335 (John Strickland); Calamy, I, pp228-9, II, pp512-6; Matthews, pp230, 418; Swayne, pp238, 239, 243

34 TNA PROB 11/23 (Henry Acton); 11/27 (Joan Peerse); 11/25 (Mercy Byrkhede); 11/28 (John Hawles); 11/304 (John Butcher); 11/310 (George Mervyn); 11/308 (Richard Phelps), 11/322 (John Ivie); 11/331 (Thomas Hancocke)

From Salisbury Bus Station to Massachusetts: an unexpected journey

John Chandler

Since 1939, when it was memorably opened by Edith Olivier brandishing a pair of grape scissors, Salisbury bus station has performed a vital function for citizens and country–dwellers.[1] Its continuous use has also preserved for almost 75 years a large open area very close to the city's medieval heart and, one hopes, a site of considerable archaeological potential when the last bus has departed. This paper makes a start, working back from 1939 and using documentary and cartographic sources, at unravelling its history, and that of its neighbours, which together occupy the northern half of Three Swans Chequer.

This research was begun under a misapprehension. I became aware that the Kithead Trust (a road transport archive maintained by enthusiasts) held deeds extending back to the 17th century of Wilts & Dorset Motor Services' property in Salisbury.[2] On inspection, I discovered that all the early documents related to land at the northern end of Castle Street and Endless Street, where the company has its garage and depot, and not to the bus station site. They are thus of some interest, but not for the present inquiry. In fact most source material, as one would expect, is in the Wiltshire and Swindon History Centre.

Salisbury bus station occupies two tenements fronting Endless Street (8 and 10) and the corresponding three fronting Rollestone Street (13, 15, 17). It adjoins on its northern side two interesting corner tenements, 12 Endless Street and 19 Rollestone Street. It is these seven premises with which this paper is mainly concerned; the southern neighbours are not considered, except to point out one little trap for the unwary. The former Woolpack Inn, 6 Endless Street, which traded between 1939 and 1974 or later,[3] was an impostor. Before the bus station it stood next door, at 8 Endless Street, and was demolished to build the block that

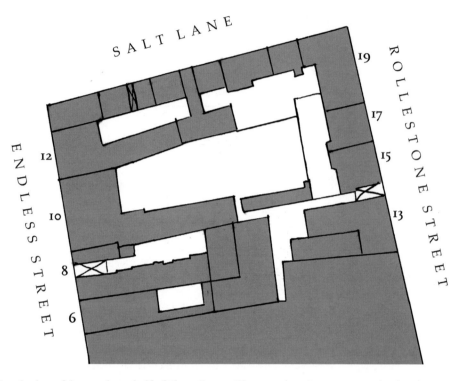

SALT LANE

ENDLESS STREET

ROLLESTONE STREET

19

17

15

13

12

10

8

6

Sketch plan of the northern half of Three Swans Chequer showing street numbering (property boundaries as existing in 1880s).

houses the bus enquiry office.[4] The old Woolpack, therefore, is part of the story.

The most substantial building demolished to create the bus station was 10 Endless Street, a seven– or eight–bay house which since 1882 had housed St Michael's Home for Friendless Girls.[5] This was a religious hostel, one of a number established in towns and cities in the wake of the 1870s social purity movement of Ellice Hopkins and other reformers. They targeted 'juvenile girls on the brink of dissipation' rather than those who had already 'fallen',[6] and St Michael's was the result of an initiative taken by the Salisbury Diocesan Deaconesses' Institution, who superintended it.[7] In 1901 it housed 15 girls, mostly from Wiltshire and Dorset, aged between 13 and 18.[8] The house had previously been a girls' school, run by Marianne Toovey and her daughters, who had moved there from Castle Street before 1861.[9]

Behind this house, and hidden from view, was a large garden, which extended beyond the centre–line of the chequer, as far as the smaller gardens behind 15 and 17 Rollestone Street. In fact 17 had been purchased by Marianne Toovey's husband John in 1871, and he was living, an elderly widower, in 15 in 1881, the

Salisbury Bus Station

Detail from an aerial photograph of Salisbury, taken before the demolition of buildings to create the bus station. Endless Street runs from bottom right to centre left.

year of his death.[10] The Tooveys and their school, therefore, probably occupied in the 1870s nearly all the land which would become the bus station 60 years later. Their predecessor in the large house, 10 Endless Street, was a surgeon and general practitioner, Thomas Moore, who maintained a large household – in 1851 a wife, six children and six servants. He and his lodger in 1841, George Tatum, were both consultant staff at Salisbury Infirmary.[11]

In our journey back from the bus station's opening we have covered a century, to the beginning of Victoria's reign. During this time the corner tenements to its north underwent various changes also. The house which survives, 12 Endless Street, was then in use as the city police station, having been purchased in 1883 to replace premises in New Canal.[12] It was fitted out with cells in 1884 and further alterations were made in 1909. Before its purchase by the city council, and right back to 1810, it had operated as a bank, which had traded under various names and with various principals, of whom Joseph Everett, one of its founders, will shortly become important in this account.[13] The bank, by then the Salisbury Old Bank of John and William Pinckney, removed to the market place in 1878 and took with it from Endless Street the fine oak panelling that had impressed the bank's customers.[14]

The corner of Endless Street and Salt Lane in 2013, showing (right to left) the bus station exit; the former police station, weights and measures department, and fire station; with older buildings beyond. Photograph by the author.

Running along Salt Lane from the Endless Street corner towards Rollestone Street was a row of small buildings, some of which survive. The corner (with surviving datestone in Roman numerals over the door) was redeveloped in 1935 by the city council to house its weights and measures department and, behind, it, the latest of several extensions and adaptations to the city fire station.[15] This started life as the volunteer fire brigade's engine house before 1898, was rebuilt in 1906, and enlarged with an ambulance station when the city took responsibility around the time of the First World War.[16] Further along, at the Rollestone Street corner, was (and is) a building which housed Miss Catherine Harrison's girls' school in the Edwardian era, and later the headquarters of the cycling club.[17]

Joseph Hague Everett, who started the bank, had died in 1818, and his premises passed to partners in his firm.[18] He was a scion of the Heytesbury dynasty of clothiers, who for decades had operated a string of mills in the Upper Wylye valley.[19] He too was an innovative clothier, and in 1803 he patented 'Salisbury Angola Moleskin', a mixed fabric of woollen and cotton, linen, silk or other yarn, woven to give the appearance of velvet.[20] He had purchased the premises in Endless Street in 1798 from the weavers' company, successor to the medieval guild of weavers, and the deed conveying it to him (very conveniently for us) defined on a carefully drawn plan the extent of his purchase and the layout of its buildings, and also described what changes had occurred to them during the previous 30 years.[21] He had become the owner, in fact, of the whole of the northern end of the chequer, including what became the bus station.

The deed with its plan tells us an interesting and complicated story, which needs only a summary here. It will be simplest to regard his acquisition as four

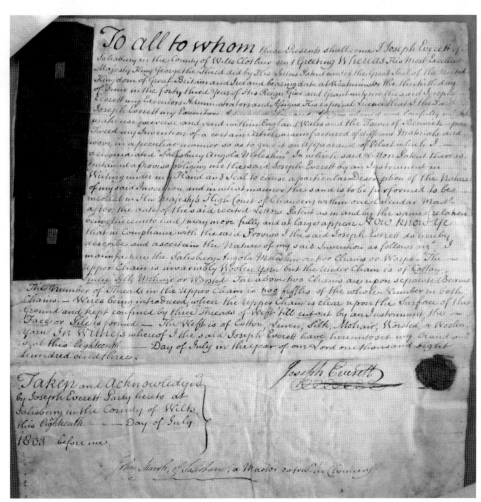

Joseph Everett's patent for Salisbury Angola Moleskin (WSA 2700/1, courtesy of Wiltshire and Swindon History Centre).

properties, the later 10 Endless Street (bus station exit), 12 Endless Street (police station, etc), 19 Rollestone Street (Miss Harrison's school), and 15–17 Rollestone Street (two cottages, now the bus station entrance). The measurements given on the plan, incidentally, suggest that these have fossilised four standard medieval tenements, of 7 x 3 perches (c35 x 15 m), as set out in the bishop's foundation charter of 1227.[22] The two cottages, 15–17 Rollestone Street, were newly erected in 1767, according to the deed, and Naish's map of Salisbury (1716) seems to confirm this by depicting a gap in the houses fronting the street at this point.[23] They may not, of course, have been the first buildings on the site, but only archaeology will determine this, and we cannot take their story further at present.

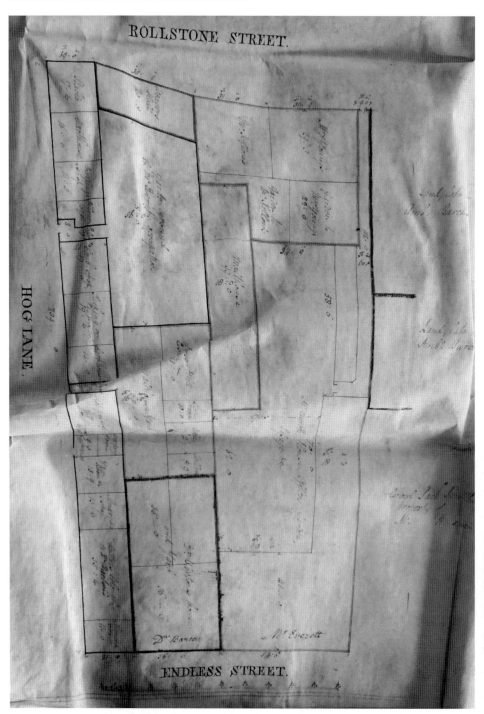

Plan attached to a deed of 1798 conveying the weavers' company premises to Joseph Everett (WSA 1214/33, courtesy of Wiltshire and Swindon History Centre).

Salisbury Bus Station

The corner of Salt Lane and Rollestone Street in 2013, showing the former girls' school and later cycling club headquarters, with the bus station entrance to its left. Photograph by the author.

The house, 10 Endless Street, demolished for the bus station, had a large garden behind it extending back almost to these cottages, and this is where the buses now park. A malthouse had been built along one side of the garden but, this apart, the area has probably been little disturbed for at least 250 years, and so should preserve an interesting archaeological sequence. The deed tells us that this house and garden had been leased by the weavers to Joseph Everett's father, William, in 1780, and it implies that Joseph had lived there since his marriage in 1788. It also recites a string of previous owners – Francis Mercer, then Samuel Case senior and Samuel Case junior – which takes us right back to 1682, when Francis Mercer paid highways rates for it.[24] He still lived there in 1690 when his household consisted of three men, one maid and three 'tablers', or lodgers;[25] but in 1699 the house was empty,[26] and by 1720 Samuel Case was the occupant.[27] In 1740 we know that he, or perhaps by then his namesake nephew, described as a clothier, rebuilt the house, because in that year he made a legal agreement with the owner of the Woolpack Inn next door about the party wall between them, which his newly erected house had evidently been built against and relied on for its stability.[28]

Samuel Case the nephew, having settled in his new house (10 Endless Street), in due course wished to expand, and in 1752 agreed with the weavers to take a lease on the house next door, which happened to be their guildhall, and the adjoining buildings along Salt Lane, with the proviso that, although there had been some alterations and he proposed more, they could continue to have access to their hall.[29] After Case died and William Everett took a new lease on the property in 1780, the dual use of the hall, by Everett and the weavers, must have become irksome, and Everett proposed a solution. He agreed with the weavers to build them a new hall, with a buttery or pantry and a necessary house – everything they needed for their feasts – on the opposite corner of the chequer, 19 Rollestone Street, so that he could have sole use of their old hall.[30] This new hall, which as we have seen became Miss Harrison's school and is still standing, was opened in June 1784;[31] its present owners, Salisbury Cycling and Social Club, have adorned it with a commemorative plaque, which unfortunately has transposed the digits of the year to 1748.

So now we have established construction dates, between 1740 and 1784, for all the principal buildings that were standing on the four ancient tenements sold by the weavers to Joseph Everett in 1798, and which were still standing until the bus station was constructed – except one. The exception is the building on the site of the weavers' hall, 12 Endless Street. The Royal Commission survey assigned it a mid–18th century origin, but much altered, and its English Heritage listing records it as late–18th century.[32] But there is little in the very full documentary record to suggest demolition and rebuilding, or even major alteration, in the 18th century. A deed of 1836, however, tells us that it had then recently been enlarged, extending for 57ft 3in along its Endless Street frontage; and this, if taken at face value, offers an approximate date for the surviving façade.[33] The implication must be that, like many other apparently 18th– or 19th–century houses in the city, disguised behind its façade and now wrecked by later use as a bank and police station, there lurked a much older structure, the guildhall of one of the most important institutions of medieval Salisbury, the weavers' guild.[34]

Almost no records are known to survive of the weavers' guild, or its successor after 1612, the weavers' company, and most information about it is derived obliquely from other sources.[35] It is perhaps a reasonable assumption that both Samuel Case and William Everett, its lessees in the 18th century, were prominent members, since both were clothiers, but it is evident that by this date the company itself was in terminal decline. Of their hall, however, some detailed information survives in deeds. A lease of 1695 lists its facilities: the hall, the two parlours next the street, the parlour within the hall, the buttery in the hall, the kitchen, the two larders within the kitchen, the malting floor on the south side of the court, the boiling room next to the cistern, the use of the pump, backside court and house of office, with ingress and egress and access to lay beer in the buttery before their feasts.[36] A slightly later lease, in 1711, goes further, providing a schedule of fixtures and fittings, down to the window glass, benches, wainscot, locks and keys.[37]

In this journey back in time the documentary record is now running out, so far as the history of the actual buildings on the site is concerned. But there is plenty more to learn about the people who lived there. The weavers' hall lessee in 1695 was Arthur Batt, and his neighbour in Endless Street, as we have discovered, was Francis Mercer. Batt, a clothier who died in 1705,[38] seems to have succeeded his father and brother, William senior and junior, between 1682 and 1686.[39] Mercer is recorded in 1688 as a brewer,[40] and may be the same as a taxpayer in Dolphin chequer in 1667.[41] His predecessor as William Batt's neighbour seems to have been Francis Dove, another brewer,[42] who paid land tax on weavers' property in the chequer in 1661,[43] and purchased the Woolpack and adjoining property in the same year.[44] He, or a son, was described as a landowner and weavers' tenant there in 1667,[45] although Francis had died, perhaps of plague, in the previous year.[46]

Besides being neighbours, and sharing aerobatic surnames, the Batts and the Doves were almost certainly related. Both families included prominent puritan leaders associated with St Edmund's church and vestry during the city's anarchic years of poverty and disease in the 1620s and 1630s; and Francis Dove was city mayor in 1644 and 1649, as was a son of his brother–in–law, Christopher Batt, in 1658.[47] Dove was a close friend of the radical minister of St Edmunds, Peter Thatcher, and when Thatcher died in 1641, Dove married his widow, Alice, who was Batt's sister.[48] Christopher Batt, worn down no doubt by civic strife and religious opposition, sailed to Massachusetts in 1638 and was one of the original 12 founders of the settlement beside the Merrimac river which, through his agency, was renamed Salisbury soon after it was established. He died in Boston in 1661, accidentally shot by one of his sons who had accompanied him to the new world. Francis Dove followed Christopher to America, probably in 1639, and became (and remained) a stakeholder in the new puritan colony, but soon returned to Salisbury, England.[49]

One day, when all the probate and property transactions that survive from medieval Salisbury have been analysed and placed in topographical order, it may be possible to continue this entangled story back another three centuries.[50] We know, for instance, that Richard Gage, an alderman and leading cloth merchant and property–owner in early 15th–century Salisbury, left land in Endless Street to the weavers' guild in his will of 1433.[51] This may have been for the site of their guildhall, although the guild had existed from 1412 or earlier, and Gage was probably one of its stewards in 1421.[52] Alice Sime was the weavers' neighbour to the south of their Endless Street property, and so was perhaps the occupant of the bus station site. She lived in a tenement which belonged to Richard Pyle, son of Robert Pyle,[53] and by 1455 he had sold it to a merchant, John Wyoth.[54] Like most sites in Salisbury the bus station still has many secrets about its past to yield up to the diligent historian and archaeologist.[55]

John Chandler is Editor of the Gloucestershire Victoria County History*, but most of his long local history career has been concerned with Salisbury and Wiltshire, about which he has written, lectured and published extensively.*

Abbreviations and Bibliography

TNA = The National Archives

WSA = Wiltshire and Swindon Archives, at the Wiltshire and Swindon History Centre, Chippenham

VCH = Victoria County History

WAM = Wiltshire Archaeological and Natural History Society Magazine

Carr, D R, 2001, *First general entry book of the city of Salisbury,* Wilts Record Society, volume 54

Chandler, J, 1983, *Endless Street,* Hobnob Press

Haskins, C, 1912, *Ancient trade guilds and companies of Salisbury*, Bennett Bros

Hatcher, H, 1843, *Old and New Sarum, or Salisbury*, Nichols

Hoyt, D W, 1897, *Old families of Salisbury and Amesbury, Massachusetts,* Providence

Kelly's Directories of Wiltshire and Salisbury, various editions

Morris, C and Waller, 2006, *A Definitive history of Wilts & Dorset Motor Services,* Hobnob Press

Neville, E, 1910, Salisbury. A Royal Aid and Supply for 1667, *WAM,* Volume 36 (for 1909–1910)

Neville, E, 1911, Salisbury in 1455 (Liber Niger), *WAM,* Volume 37 (for 1911–1912)

Newman, R and Howells, J, 2001, *Salisbury Past,* Phillimore

Olivier, E, 1941, *Country moods and tenses*, B T Batsford

Royal Commission on Historical Monuments (England), *Ancient and historical monuments in the city of Salisbury*, 1, 1980, HMSO [RCHM]

Rogers, K H, 1976, *Wiltshire and Somerset Woollen Mills*, Pasold

Slack, P, 1975, *Poverty in Early Stuart Salisbury,* Wilts Record Society, volume 31

Walkowitz, J R, 1982, *Prostitution and Victorian Society,* Cambridge University Press

Notes

1   Morris and Waller, 44; Olivier, 67–8
2   Kithead Trust, De Salis Drive, Hampton Lovett, Droitwich Spa WR9 0QE. I am most grateful to Peter Jaques of the Trust for permitting me to examine the archives.
3   *Kelly's Directory of Salisbury*, 1974, 148
4   Morris and Waller, 43
5   Newman and Howells, aerial photograph, c1930 as rear endpaper; *Kelly's directory of Wiltshire*, 1907 and later editions
6   Walkowitz, 238–9
7   *Salisbury Diocesan Gazette*, 1888 edition, 16–17. I owe this reference to Dr Jane Howells
8   TNA RG 13/1954, ff116v, 117
9   TNA HO 107/1847, f7; RG 9/1317, f41; RG 11/2072, f33
10 Kithead Trust, schedule of deeds of 17 Rollestone St; TNA RG 11/2072, f35
11 TNA HO 107/1190/3, f24; Salisbury General Hospital, 1967, *Salisbury 200*, 158–9

12 WSA G23/152/3

13 Haskins, 97

14 *Ibid*; *Kelly's Directory of Wiltshire,* 1885, 240

15 WSA G23/152/12

16 WSA G23/701/30 (loose sketch dated 1903); *Kelly's Directory of Wiltshire* (various editions)

17 *Kelly's Directory of Wiltshire,*1903 and later editions

18 WSA 1214/33, deed of 10 February 1834

19 Rogers, 238, 240–1, 244–7

20 WSA 2700/1

21 WSA 1214/33, deed of 16 February 1798

22 Hatcher, 728; discussion in Chandler, 27, 285

23 RCHM, plate16

24 WSA 1901/224

25 WSA G23/1/181

26 *Ibid*

27 WSA G23/1/185

28 WSA 776/1059, agreement 12 April 1740

29 WSA 1214/33, deed of 16 February 1798; WSA 1214/32, leases 1752, 1766

30 WSA 1214/33, deed of 16 February 1798

31 Haskins, 95, citing *Salisbury Journal* 28 June 1784; *VCH Wilts*, 6, 137

32 RCHM, 135 (monument 347); National Heritage List, 1023648

33 WSA 1214/34. The measurement corresponds with that given on the 1798 plan of 12 Endless Street's frontage continued to the corner of the street

34 From an inspection of the interior it seems that nothing now survives of this earlier building. I am grateful to Andrew Minting for investigating.

35 *VCH Wilts*, 6, 133, 137; Haskins, 91–7. The weavers did not reform in the same way as the other guilds, and a charter of 1590, reciting an earlier one of 1562, is extant: WSA G23/1/245PC

36 WSA 1214/32

37 *Ibid*

38 TNA PROB 11/485/348

39 WSA 1901/224, highways rates 1682, 1686. William junior, also a clothier, predeceased his father in 1683: TNA PROB 11/373/240

40 Ellis, H, 1827, *Original letters illustrative of English history*, 2nd series, 4 , 181

41 Neville (1910), 416

42 He occurs in a list of members of the brewers' company in 1625: WSA G23/1/264, f3

43 WSA G23/1/179

44 WSA 776/1059, deed of 20 March 1661

45 Neville (1910), 422

46 Hoyt, 132–3; his tombstone apparently refers to 'that fatal year 1666'

47 Slack

48 Hoyt, 60, 133. The families are to be found on numerous American genealogical websites. For more information about Thatcher see Claire Cross's paper in this issue.

49 Hoyt, 59–60, 132–3

50   See comments in *Sarum Chronicle* 12, 2012, 81–6

51   *VCH Wilts* 6, 133; TNA PROB 11/3/497; WSA G23/1/215, f8, p14

52   Carr, pp 46, 100

53   WSA G23/1/215, f8, p14

54   Neville (1911), 82

55   My thanks to Steven Hobbs and Andrew Minting for their help on archival and architectural matters.